eco-chic
weddings

eco-chic weddings

Simple Tips to Plan an Environmentally Friendly, Socially Responsible, Affordable, and Stylish Celebration

Emily Elizabeth Anderson

Hatherleigh Press

NEW YORK • LONDON

HATHERLEIGH PRESS

5-22 46th Avenue, Suite 200
Long Island City, NY 11101
www.healthylivingbooks.com

Library of Congress Cataloging-in-Publication Data
Anderson, Emily, 1948-
  Eco-chic weddings : simple tips to plan an environmentally friendly, socially responsible, affordable, and stylish celebration / Emily Anderson.
      p. cm.
  Includes bibliographical references and index.
  ISBN-10: 1-57826-240-2 (alk. paper)
  ISBN-13: 978-1-57826-240-3 (alk. paper) 1. Weddings--Planning.
2. Weddings--Equipment and supplies. I. Title.
  HQ745.A55 2007
  395.2'2--dc22

                                                    2006036602

Hatherleigh books are available for bulk purchase, special promotions, and premiums. For information on reselling and special purchase opportunities, please call us at 1-800-528-2550 and ask for the Special Sales Manager.

At Hatherleigh Press we are committed to the responsible use of natural resources. This book is one step towards that goal. It is printed on 100% recycled paper. In doing so, we have saved 45 trees, 15,000 gallons of water, 30 million BTUs of energy, two tons of greenhouse gases, and one ton of solid waste. The book is printed with vegetable-based inks.

Cover Designed by Deborah Miller and Allison Furrer
Interior Designed by Christine Weathersbee

10   9   8   7   6   5   4   3   2   1

Printed in the United States

contents

introduction: Your Wedding, Your World   1

one: Wedding Basics   11
(Where and When)

two: Engagement and Wedding Rings   21

three: Wedding Attire   31

four: Wedding Registry   47

five: Wedding Invitation   55

six: Flowers, Style, and Design   63

seven: Wedding Favors   77

eight: Health and Beauty   83

nine: Menu   89

ten: Transportation   97

eleven: Honeymoon   103

twelve: Married Life   113

acknowledgments   125

appendix   Eco-Chic Resources   127

Dedication

For my husband
David

And in memory of my mother
Betsy

Introduction

your wedding, your world

Welcome to Eco-Chic Weddings. I'm glad you're here. Eco-chic is the belief that you can have a beautiful, stylish, well-designed life, and also make good consumer choices. Choices that will benefit the environment and society, as opposed to purchasing items that are produced at the expense of under-paid or mistreated workers, or were made using a toxic or damaging production process. _Eco-Chic Weddings_ is the first comprehensive guide for the soon-to-be-married set interested in making chic, stylish buying decisions that are also eco-minded and socially responsible. Eco-chic buying decisions, to be specific. And as the amount of money spent on weddings increases year by year, more and more products and services are available for these couples. And the growth in weddings each year is indeed dramatic—there have been 200 million more weddings in the past year than there were in the year 2000.

According to a recent survey by The Condé Nast Bridal Group, the amount of money we spend on weddings has increased by 100% since 1990.

There are many possible reasons for this increase in wedding spending. Books and magazines encourage us to create special, unique events for our families and friends. Indeed, for many people, planning a wedding can be one of the most creative, exciting projects in their lives. Choosing the colors, the dress, the flowers—this is a lot of fun, and it isn't something most of us get to do on a regular basis.

While the wedding business has become such a prevalent part of today's marketplace, there has also been another consumer-trend taking place—the eco-friendly, sustainable movement. With the popularity of the "green" movement, every day we see more and more options and ideas that are environmentally and socially conscious, ideas with style and integrity. And yes, many of the ideas are perfectly suited for your wedding. *Eco-Chic Weddings* has gathered these ideas, products, and resources to make it easy for you to make your wedding as environmentally responsible, socially aware, and eco-chic as possible. Because I believe that you can have it all—the look and the style that you want, and better choices about where you spend your money that help you feel good about how you impact the global community. Planning your wedding is a great time to make the decision to be more sustainable—the decisions you make now can continue into your married life, when and if you become parents, and so on. *Eco-Chic Weddings* sees this moment in your life as the ideal time to take a critical look at your purchasing choices, where your dollars are going, and your impact on the world. The goal of this book is to help you lay a solid groundwork for your future by guiding you through the wedding planning process. This book will answer two very important questions: WHY should you have an eco-chic wedding, and HOW can you be eco-chic?

Well, we all know that planning a wedding means spending money. The average cost of the American wedding is now $27,825 (in 1990, it was $15,208). So let's take a quick look at where you might be spending your cash:

Reception	42%
Engagement/Wedding Rings	20%
Honeymoon	12%
Photo/Video	8%
Bride and Groom's Apparel	7%
Flowers	7%
Invitations	5%
Cake	3%
Music (Ceremony/Reception)	3%
Ceremony	1%
Transportation	1%

Based on this breakdown, most couples spend the largest portion of their dollars on the Reception, but a hefty sum is also spent on just the engagement ring. In the three categories—Reception, Rings, and the Honeymoon—the total amount spent on weddings in the U.S. are:

Honeymoons	$8 billion
Diamond Engagement Rings	$7 billion
Wedding Registries	$19 billion

[Source: Condé Nast Bridal Group—American Wedding Study 2006]

You might be shocked to learn that, according to a recent survey by the Fairchild Bridal Group, wedding spending in the U.S. has gone from $5 billion in 2002 to $125 billion in 2005, with 295 million wedding guests attending the nation's 2.1 million weddings this year. It stands to reason that weddings have a unique impact on the environment and the global economy. So while you may think that this is a really bad time for you to be a responsible global citizen, it actually is the perfect time. Perfect because you are planning your wedding, but you're also planning your future—so many decisions are being made, such as where you will live, how you will live, what sort of things you will have in your new married life.

This is the deal—as we, the consumer, demonstrate a demand for more sustainable products in the marketplace, businesses will pay attention, and wanting to get our business, they will be encouraged to adopt better, healthier ways of producing and selling goods. Some people refer to this as "voting with your pocketbook," which is exactly what it is. You, bride- or groom-to-be, can start by choosing products for your wedding made by companies and countries that practice conscious commerce, that participate in fair trade, and who are making a difference in the world—whether through making contributions to environmental efforts or supporting emerging economies. And selfishly, this will be a better, healthier path for you to take, because your unique, non-typical choices will result in a wedding that truly is a reflection of who you are, what your values are, and what you believe in. It is my hope that this book will help you see that there really isn't a right or a wrong way to have a wedding—what it all comes down to is personal choice. With *Eco-Chic Weddings*, I offer to you the simplest ideas that you can incorporate into your wedding, so that you, busy bride or groom, don't have to do a lot of work to make a difference.

To help you make eco-chic decisions as you plan the wedding of your dreams, this book is organized into 3 key areas: ways to reduce, ways to reuse, and ways to recycle. Thus, each chapter includes simple ways to reduce your impact on the environment, such as not wasting food or simplifying the amount of flower arrangements you have; how to select items that can be reused after the wedding, such as selecting shoes you can wear for other occasions after the wedding (go ahead, get those Manolos if you will wear them for years to come); and finally, ways to recycle items you use at the wedding or how you can purchase items that have been recycled, such as using recycled paper for your invitations or purchasing a vintage dress you have a seamstress refashion to suit your style.

Each person on the planet has their own "footprint" that represents the amount of energy they consume, waste they produce, and impact their buying decisions make on the global community. By choosing sustainable products, fair-trade items, or locally produced goods, you can reduce your individual "footprint." You can reduce the amount you consume by simplifying your choices, staying within your budget, avoiding going into debt, and reusing items you purchase for your wedding rather than buying one-time-use things. An example of a one-time-use item would be wedding shoes you will only wear once and then throw away. You can also ensure that items used for your wedding are recycled, rather than thrown away. Let's talk about specific ways you can Reduce, Reuse, and Recycle for your wedding.

Reduce

According to the EPA (Environmental Protection Agency), the U.S. is producing more landfill waste now than ever before. One estimate shows that between the years 1960 and 1997, total U.S. Municiple trash, or landfill waste, increased an astounding 146.5%. What are some basic ways you can reduce the amount of trash you produce?

- **Simplify:** Whenever you can, wherever you can, without compromising your style, know that fewer details to attend to will translate into more fun, more time for your guests, less stress, and less over-consumption. Avoid buying products with excess packaging, including gifts—did you know you can request no wrapping paper for your gifts?
- **Be an Individual:** Opt out of the idea that you "have" to do anything—for example, the wedding favor. The often-tacky, one-time-use wedding favors have become commonplace, and 99.9% of the time, the guests toss the favor in the trash post-event. I myself did not give my guests a favor; instead, we made a donation to Habitat for Humanity. Upon arrival, our guests read about this donation on a little sign at the seating card table, which made them smile, and that is something they won't throw away.
- **Prioritize:** Decide what your priorities are and where you want to focus your resources. Want that fabulous Carmen Marc Valvo? Then maybe you can reduce in other areas—the flowers or your transportation. Whatever you do, don't go into debt for the sake of having an over-the-top wedding. For instance, I made sure to choose a location that had a décor we found pleasing, eliminating the need to spend extra money, time, and resources decorating the space.

Reuse

When you buy items that can be reused in their present form, you are practicing what experts refer to as the "cradle to cradle" philosophy: Make sure what you purchase can be reused and is of good quality so as to have a long and useful life. Important steps you can take to reuse as much as possible:

- **Borrow:** Check to see if you can use borrowed, rented, or secondhand items before you purchase new ones. I borrowed a beautiful pearl bracelet from my good friend Tara—which was even more special because she couldn't be at the wedding.
- **Make Style a Priority:** Timeless, classic design is an excellent way to select items for your wedding that won't go out of style.
- **Avoid Wedding-Themed Items:** For more than one reason, not the least of which is the fact that "wedding" items (shoes, bags, shawls, etc.) automatically cost more money than non-wedding items. Another reason to avoid wedding-centric goods: with almost 100% certainty, you will never use that item again. Stick to pretty, tasteful, well-designed items that are perfect for a "wedding" because you say they are.

Recycle

Recycling is the process of making something new out of an old item or material, such as turning discarded wine bottles into drinking glasses, or taking an old wedding dress and remaking it into a new design. Buildings and other structures can also be recycled, such as turning an old school into a hotel, or transforming a trolley car into a bus. Be a champion of recycling and follow these basic tenets:

- **Check for the Recycling Label:** Buy recycled products and products that are made out of recyclable materials. Always check for the recycled/recyclable label.
- **Set a Good Example:** Ensure your reception location, florist, caterer, and anyone else involved with producing your wedding practices good recycling behavior.
- **Support Businesses Doing the Right Thing:** You can make a positive contribution to sustainable business simply by hosting your wedding at a venue that has been recycled, such as a mansion that is now operating as a family restaurant. You can also support designers who use their ingenuity to recycle non-virgin resources, such as one-of-a-kind journals as wedding favors, which have been made from recycled books, or even your great-aunt's wedding dress that a talented seamstress has recreated to be your own unique design.

Eco-Chic Resources:
Getting Started

Organic Weddings   http://organicweddings.com

Michelle Kozin was ahead of the curve when she published her book a number of years ago.

Green Weddings, California   http://greenweddings.net

An online resource, based in California, with links to a variety of green wedding resources

Conscious Consumer Marketplace http://www.newdream.org

The Center for a New American Dream's Conscious Consumer Marketplace makes it easier for you to buy environmentally and socially responsible items for your wedding—and for your life.

Zerofootprint   http://zerofootprint.net

Information, products, and services for green consumers

More Hip Than Hippie   http://morehipthanhippie.com

Resources for a cool green lifestyle

Great Green Weddings   http://greatgreenwedding.com

An eco-minded wedding site with information about everything from wedding favors to honeymoons.

Choose to Reuse

Written by Nikki Goldbeck and David Goldbeck

An Encyclopedia of Services, Businesses, Tools & Charitable Programs That Facilitate Reuse

Cradle to Cradle

Written by William McDonough and Michael Braungart

This book offers compelling examples of corporations that are not just doing less harm—they're actually doing some good for the environment and their neighborhoods, and making more money in the process.

chapter 1

wedding basics
(where and when)

It may seem that you barely get to enjoy the engagement before you jump headfirst into the planning. This sense of urgency comes from the fact that, if you do have a specific location in mind, you'll want to reserve it as soon as you are able. One way to avoid putting this immediate pressure on yourself is to be as flexible as possible about where and when you get married. If you keep an open mind, as I did, you just may end up with everything you want.

According to the Bridal Consultants of America, October is now the most popular month of the year, perhaps because it tends to be a more pleasant temperature than June or September (some speculate that this may be due to global warming trends). If you are willing to be flexible, you will be pleasantly surprised to learn that off-season rates and availability are a serious bargain. I for one believe that anytime of the year is the perfect time to get married, so just keep an open mind to the unexpected possibilities.

Indoor, outdoor, rooftop, garden. Beach, boat, or the top of a mountain. It seems the list of where to get married is endless. Or perhaps you have a destination wedding in mind—a trend which has seen a 400% increase over the past 15 years. Wherever you look, consider your reception locale very carefully—I suggest that you make a commitment to avoid the wedding factory. I consider any location that hosts multiple weddings during a day, often at the same time, to be a "wedding factory." These places tend to boast "one-stop-shopping" prices, but what you end up getting is something that feels more like a convention than a uniquely special experience.

As a former event planner, I can tell you that a wedding is basically no different than an event, which is how I approached planning my wedding. Thus, you don't have to sign up for things that only have the "wedding" stamp on them; there are many other places out there that

a wedding in the jungle

Meredith Haberfeld and Robert Weil gave their guests more than a party—their wedding was an adventure in a virtually untouched part of the world; an all-inclusive, once-in-a-lifetime trip to the rainforest of Costa Rica. Meredith and Robert invited a few select friends and family to their nuptials on the Osa Peninsula, which is in the southwestern region of the country, just above Panama. About as eco-chic a location as you can get, the Costa Rican government designated 100,000 acres of the peninsula as the Corcovado National Park. The Osa Peninsula has high levels of biodiversity, hosts a rich array of fauna including jaguar, you can use to host a wedding. Considering you will spend almost half of your entire budget on this location, choose a place that you feel connected to, that has a staff you like, and hopefully is connected to the local community, because supporting local business is an important aspect of the eco-chic lifestyle. The restaurant where I had my wedding was a local family-owned establishment. They hosted weddings and other events, but they are also one of the areas best-known restaurants. Because it was a family-owned establishment, the staff made me and my family feel like their family. They took a special interest in making sure the day went off without a hitch, and it did. If you do "go local," meaning, you spend your dollars at a local business, your funds will in turn be re-invested directly into the local economy.

Okay, so you may want to do the big event in the beautiful outdoors—sunny skies, lovely breezes, sun-kissed cheeks. Who doesn't dream of having their wedding outside? Especially if you really are a nature-loving gal or guy. Well, it may sound lovely to have a mid-afternoon wedding in

the Central American squirrel monkey, the Baird's tapir, and three species of sea turtles. More than 375 bird species are found on the Osa Peninsula, including the country's largest population of the threatened scarlet macaw. Osa is also home to the harpy eagle and the yellow-billed cotinga. Miles of the peninsula serve as a nature preserve. In addition to being surrounded by the amazing creatures that inhabit the peninsula, Meredith and Robert were joined by twenty of their closest friends. The couple and their guests enjoyed delicious tropical food, native dancers to entertain them, and a peaceful honeymoon in a lodge nestled into the cliffs over the ocean.

the beautiful backyard of your childhood home, but what will that really cost you and the environment? From tent rental, to parking, to the wear and tear on your mother's prized rose garden, you might be surprised at the high cost of having a wedding at home. Ovens, dishes, glasses, chairs, and tables all need to be rented, which drives the cost up faster than anything else. Likewise, taking that gondola to the top of your favorite Colorado ski top might sound like the perfect way to commune with nature, but what happens once you and 250 of your closest friends get to the top? Well, all of the food, cooking equipment, chairs, tables, lighting, and sound equipment need to be sent up the mountain as well. And believe me, you will definitely be charged a premium for the effort. Open your mind to the alternative possibilities for where to have your wedding. You don't have to follow the leader, and you don't have to reinvent the wheel either. Many places may have hosted parties or other events, maybe not a wedding, but perhaps they would be open to the idea of hosting yours.

Wedding Venue Checklist

- Ask to see photos from other weddings, to see where flowers might go, and how the rooms can be arranged.
- Does your venue plan to host other events at the same time?
- Ask if you can choose your own vendors.
- Does the venue have off peak rates?
- What is their recycling policy?
- Do they participate in any community support programs (such as a community garden, workforce development, mentoring programs, green business initiatives)?

- Where do they purchase their food, and do they support local or regional farmers?
- Can you bring in your own wine (not only can you opt for organic labels, but often the cost is lower if you bring in your own alcohol, but check to see if they charge what is called a "corkage fee")?
- Is the venue a part of a larger chain or is it independently owned? If it is a part of a chain, do you believe in the business ethics of the larger company?
- Do they compost leftover food? If not, is there a local garden that they can donate all leftovers to (because of food safety regulations, restaurants cannot donate food once it has been prepared for service)?
- Will you have a staff member designated as your wedding coordinator? This person will direct the wedding day events and make sure all of your wishes are followed.
- If you plan for an outdoor wedding, is there a good indoor option in case of rain?
- Can you host both your ceremony and your reception at this location?
- Are you able to use your own baker in case you wish to have an organically baked cake?
- What décor elements does the site have, such as linens, cake plates, vases, compote bowls, etc.?
- Does the venue have a list of recommended vendors with whom they have worked in the past and who they know will do a good job?
- As you get close to your date, check to see if there are any events directly before or right after your event.

• Is it possible to use flower arrangements from the event before your wedding, or even from the night before, for things like the entrance table, or the front porch, or the restrooms? Hey, maybe you can even contact the people and join forces—you never know, they might have fantastic taste in flowers!

If possible, choose a business that is enriching the lives of the local community and embracing green business practices. Ask the management questions about their business choices (do they recycle? do they compost? do they work with local farmers, or do they have their own garden?). Follow these suggestions, and you will end up with something that is much more unique and tasteful and has more of the elements that are important to you. At the very least, choose a place that will work with you to find the solutions and the special details that will make this day yours and yours alone—with eco-chic style.

Reduce

• **Choose a Place with Style:** In the spirit of simplicity and making an effort to reduce consumption, choose a place, whether it's a church or a synagogue, that is aesthetically pleasing to you. By doing so you will eliminate the need to spend time and money decorating the space. Simple flowers, which can be repurposed for use at the reception, might just be enough if you find the right place, particularly since all eyes will be on you and your betrothed.

• **Support Businesses Doing Good:** Find out what efforts they are making to be sustainable, improve their business standards as they relate to the environment and local economies in which they operate. For example, the Six Senses Resorts and Spas is an international company with resorts in Southeast Asia and parts of Europe. Their mission is to work in harmony with the local environments and people, supporting and sustaining natural resources.

- **Be Wary of Going Outdoors:** The stereotypical eco-friendly wedding might be outdoors, but before you step outside consider whether or not you will need to have pest-control to ensure that your guests are comfortable. The most popular form of insect repellent available to consumers in the U.S. is diethyl-meta-toluamide, "DEET." Another pest-control used is Malathion. Both of these have raised some health concerns. Malathion is chemically related to nerve gas, and it works by disrupting nervous system processes in insects, and also affects humans. It has also been linked to cancer and other nervous system disorders. A healthier alternative would be to use BTI, a naturally occurring organism that poses no health threat to humans or wildlife.

- **Do Everything in One Place:** Hosting your ceremony and reception at the same location is one way to make your life less complicated, as well as reducing the amount of transportation pollution associated with your wedding.

Reuse

- **Use a Non-Typical Wedding Venue:** Many colleges and universities have chapels on campus, as well as reception areas perfectly suited to a wedding reception. If you can, use your alma mater and you'll probably get a deal on the price. Your parents, friends, or siblings may have a connection you haven't thought of yet. And you can feel good about supporting an institution of higher learning. There might even be a high school or art school that you can use as a venue, such as the Cranbrook School in Bloomfield Hills, Michigan. Cranbrook sits on a beautiful 315-acre campus. And in Pasadena, California, there's the Art Institute, which was designed by a student of the modern architect, Ludwig Mies Van Der Rohe. Your event would certainly be chic and unique in this modern locale.

- **Find a Vineyard:** A lovely setting for both a ceremony and reception, and you will be supporting local farming and commerce. You also might get a discount on the wine. Oftentimes they'll allow you to bring in your own caterer and other vendors. You may need to put up a tent for the reception area, but if you don't mind the additional cost, this is an ideal way to celebrate your day in a way that also celebrates sustainability. As a matter of fact, many vineyards now include wedding packages. Sometimes they even have a restaurant with a chef on site, so you get the same benefit of having your reception at a restaurant.

- **Go to the Park:** Many people don't realize the great options available to them via the parks and recreation department. Even Central Park in New York City has fantastic venues within the park and historic buildings nestled amidst the flora. But if you go this route keep in mind that the facility may not have a kitchen or proper catering facilities. If so, your catering costs will jump.

- **Support a Non-Profit:** Museums, landmark buildings, and other cultural centers often have pristine gardens and historic rooms that add a level of sophistication and distinction.

Recycle

- **Use a Recycled Venue:** Community improvement locations are another option to consider. These are locations where local business owners have taken an old building, garden, or farm and refurbished them, adding to the overall aesthetic of the community. My wedding was at a mansion that had been turned into a restaurant. The rolling acres of the original home had been preserved, and it felt good to be supporting something that was an important historic part of the local community.
- **Ask About Your Venue's Recycling Practice:** Some hotels and restaurants compost their food on site and also participate in recycling programs. Ask if this is the case.

Eco-Chic Resources: Locations

Green Hotels Association   http://greenhotels.com
Lists participating eco-designated locations, both national and international destinations, to help you select a place that focuses on sustainability. Use this as a cross-reference to find out how green your venue is.

The Knot   http://theknot.com
Has a really good local venue search function, but you'll have to check on how eco-friendly specific locations are

The Wedding Channel   http://weddingchannel.com

Search for venues, small and large, state by state

Unique Venues   http://www.uniquevenues.com

Has a research function that let's you search for locations in the U.S. and abroad. You can even check for places based on capacity and proximity to an airport.

Gathering Guide   http://gatheringguide.com

Find an event location, for the ceremony and the reception, anywhere in the country.

chapter 2

engagement and wedding rings

Rubies, sapphires, emeralds. These precious stones were once the ultimate symbols of love and commitment. Only if you couldn't afford these rarer gems did you opt for a diamond ring instead. Now, some fellows are willing to spend more on the engagement ring than they might spend on a down-payment for a house. This change occurred fairly recently, probably around the time that most of our grandparents became engaged. In the 1930s, DeBeers, the largest diamond trading company in the world, launched it's famous campaign "A Diamond is Forever," and we've been buying diamonds ever since. Approximately 80% of engaged couples in the U.S. purchase diamond engagement rings, proving that the ad campaign really was one of the best ever.

faux diamonds are a girl's best friend

There are many reasons to buy a synthetic diamond engagement ring. You can opt out of the deceptive pricing and marketing perpetrated by diamond retailers, and you can keep your conscience clear knowing you aren't supporting an unsafe and unethical business. Creating a perfect synthetic diamond has long been attempted, and recently, Charles and Colvert have come as close to perfect as possible. Their diamond product, called Moissanite, is virtually undetectable to the human eye. In fact, experts say the only way to know that a Moissanite diamond hasn't been mined is because it is too perfect. Another way to tell the difference between a synthetic diamond and a mined diamond is the price. The prices of mined diamond prices are almost entirely determined by DeBeers Diamond Company. DeBeers controls the availability of diamonds throughout the world (especially in the United States), so they can keep the prices sky high. In fact, diamonds are not scarce at all. Because of this price manipulation, couples in the U.S. pay 40% too much for their diamond engagement ring. Almost half of the diamonds sold in the U.S. have been altered to increase their "value." You can opt-out of this problem-riddled business and follow the direction of socially conscious celebrities such as Gwyneth Paltrow, Kanye West, and Angelina Jolie; in response to the many problems surrounding mined diamonds, they have made the decision to wear only synthetic diamonds to the many high-profile events they attend.

My husband and I opted out of the diamond trade altogether, and instead chose to go with a watery blue aquamarine. I can't tell you how many times people compliment my ring, and I love the fact that nobody in the world has one like it. I chose an alternative gem partly because of the cost factor and also because of the controversy surrounding diamonds, or "conflict diamonds." Conflict diamonds are diamonds that originate from areas in sub-Saharan Africa that are often controlled by forces that use the profit from diamonds to fund their illegal military action—places like Sierra Leone, Angola, and other parts of Africa.

Another unfortunate consequence of the diamond market and some other precious gemstones is the exploitation of workers. Diamond miners often work in cramped and unsafe conditions in tunnels, and dust from the mines can cause respiratory diseases in workers and residents of nearby communities. The mining of colored gemstones, such as rubies and emeralds, also holds risks. Often, small-scale mining operations are unable to invest in the tools and equipment that may prevent accidents and provide healthier working conditions. Child labor is also a common problem in mining.

Another problem in the jewelry world is the fact that gold mining is currently one of the world's dirtiest industries. Did you know that the production of a single gold ring generates 20 tons of mine waste, on average? Me neither. And irresponsible gold-mining practices have been polluting water and soil with toxic chemicals, endangering the health of people and ecosystems, virtually unchecked for decades. But, as with diamonds and other gems, there are changes taking place in the industry to make it better. This is a good thing, because gold mining is vital to the fragile economies of many impoverished countries. And two-thirds of global gold production is from developing countries. So when we talk about economic development in these countries, the business of gold mining can bring substantial improvements in the quality of life of many people.

But if you have your heart set on a diamond ring, as so many brides do, you can find a good alternative to conflict diamonds and if you are a fan of gold, you can find better options. Due in part to a growing awareness of this situation in the U.S. and elsewhere, with entertainers and Hollywood A-listeners like Kanye West and Leonardo DiCaprio raising their voices, some jewelry companies are making a commitment to selling only conflict-free diamonds, and to only carry non-dirty gold. You can be fairly certain that if your diamond is mined in Canada, it's not a conflict diamond—virtually all diamonds mined in Canada are conflict-free and have been mined under safe, regulated working conditions. There are specific jewelers, such as Leber Jewelers, who continue to make a commitment to selling diamonds, gold, and other gems that have no negative eco or social impact. Leber Jewelry will not purchase Burmese rubies because they have been found to fund the military Junta in Burma. Leber has even started the Jewelers' Burma Relief Project, which works with the Foundation for the People of Burma to provide direct medical, educational, and micro-business development assistance to the Burmese. And the American Gem Trade Association (AGTA) has begun developing "best practices" for gem sourcing, showing that the conversation about where gems come from and the issues related to fair trade is growing louder.

Let's encourage this multi-billion dollar industry to continue to make the necessary changes to be more environmentally sustainable and ask your jeweler if your gold jewelry has been mined in an eco-friendly way. The U.S doesn't require a country-of-origin label on imported jewels or precious metals (yet), so you'll have to take some initiative to seek out companies who strive to be good corporate citizens. You can start at websites like nodirtygold.org, oxfam.org, or corpwatch.org.

Reduce

- **Request a Certificate of Origin:** Your retailer should be able to provide you with the background information on your diamond. This way, you can be sure you're purchasing a non-conflict diamond (often these diamonds originate from Canada). Jewelers should provide you with a meaningful guarantee that the jewelry you are buying is not tarnished with human rights abuses, environmental destruction, or conflict.
- **Consider a Faux Diamond:** There are multi-carat, gem-quality "cultured" diamonds being produced today that are so good even the big diamond companies are paying attention (Moissanite). Untraceable to the naked eye, maybe you're modern enough to shrug off convention and wear something that only you know wasn't mined in the depths of Africa.
- **Don't Buy Dirty Gold:** Only buy gold from a reputable source. For example, gold manufacturer Newmont Mining pledges that it will adhere to new standards to reduce the environmental impact of gold mining.
- **Buy American:** Mines outside U.S. borders are not subject to the same rules as in the U.S., even if run by American companies. If you purchase your gems from U.S.-based mines, you can ensure that sound business practices were followed. Plus, you'll support a local, U.S.-based business, and your gems won't have to travel as far to get to you.
- **Buy Local:** You may even go so far as to buy your gems from specific states because a handful of them have "reclamation" laws on the books calling for the safeguarding of surface and ground-water around mining operations, and cleanup and re-vegetation rules to restore mining areas to their original condition.

- **Buy One Ring:** Can you have your engagement ring serve as your wedding band as well? This is a popular trend for many brides these days who aren't afraid to buck tradition and be unique.
- **Support Companies Doing Good:** Seek out gems produced by businesses, such as the Columbia Gem House, that adhere to a set of principles that include environmental protection and fair labor practices at cutting and jewelry factories. For example, the company pays above minimum wage and offers health benefits to workers, and it has built a school for the workers' children at one specific mine. Uncut stones are sent to Columbia's Chinese cutting factory, where workers are paid three times the minimum wage and receive benefits that include room and board, food allowances, paid vacation, and medical and disability insurance. Rather than hurting the bottom line, the company's sales have increased 20–30 percent since the initiative began several years ago.

Reuse

- **Don't Buy New:** Instead, find a used ring, maybe a vintage or antique ring. You can be sure you won't see it on every other girl out there. What about your mom or grandma's diamond? Would they be willing to pass down that rock to you? Used and vintage gold wedding bands are everywhere, and you may be able to get them resized.
- **Go Online:** Don't snub online opportunities; there are people who would love to get cash for their precious jewelry. If you do buy a diamond online, be sure you get the ring certified by a reputable jeweler before you make the purchase.

• **Place an Advertisement:** With so many places to list wanted items, such as craigslist, why not put up a post for a diamond ring? You never know if there might be a jilted bride or groom just waiting for the opportunity to recoup some of their investment.

Recycle

• **Ask Around:** Does anyone in your family have an old piece of jewelry they would be willing to part with—perhaps you can have a talented jewelry designer create something new out of something old.

• **Look in Your Jewelry Box:** Do you have any old gold that can be melted and remade into a sparkling new wedding band? Take your gold jewelry to the store and ask if you can get a ring made out of it—you never know, you might even be able to design a really unique creation from that high school ring you had to have but never wore!

• **Support an Artist:** There are a number of talented artists creating jewelry out of used metal and precious stones. Look into commissioning an engagement ring, or wedding bands, with a real artisan who you can feel good about supporting in his or her creative endeavor.

Eco-Chic Resources:
Jewelry

Council for Responsible Jewellery Practices

http://responsiblejewellery.com

Founded in May 2005 by members of the jewellery industry, the organization is committed to promoting responsible business practices throughout the industry from mine to retail.

Laurel Denise   http://laureldenise.com

Handmade, custom-made jewelry pieces

There are wide-ranging social and environmental problems linked to the global jewelery supply chain—from child labor and the exploitation of indigenous people to environmental degradation and disaster.

Cred Jewellery   http://cred.tv

Committed to providing a positive fair trade alternative for jewellery that pays special attention to human rights, labor standards, and care for the environment

Brilliant Earth   http://brilliantearth.com

Sells conflict-free diamonds

Green Karat   http://greenkarat.com

Uses recycled gold for all of its jewelry. They get their precious metals from objects like used jewelry and electronics.

Leber Jewelry   http://leberjeweler.com
Sells only non-conflict, free trade, and non-dirty gold items

Lee Bell Designs   http://www.fromthesky.com
For wide selection of classic, vintage style rings with Moissanite

Sumiche Jewelry Co.   http://sumiche.com
Hand-crafted custom jewelry made from sustainable mined gold and platinum

Corporacion Oro Verde or Green Gold
                              http://greengold-oroverde.org
Sells eco-friendly wedding jewelry and considers itself to be an investment in the conservation of bio-diversity

The Signet Group   http://kay.com
                              http://www.sterlingjewelers.com
Parent company of Sterling and Kay Jewelers; pledges to sell only non-dirty gold

Vancleef and Arpels   http://www.vancleef-arpels.com
Founding member of The Council for Responsible Jewelry Practices. Other members:

   Fortunoff   http://fortunoff.com

   Cartier   http://cartier.com

   Piaget   http://www.piaget.com

   Zales   http://zales.com

Tiffany & Co.   http://www.tiffany.com

Supports the Green Gold Program through the environmental program of its foundation. They've pledged to sell only Green Gold, as well as certified non-conflict diamonds.

Seraglia Couture Gems and Jewelery   http://seraglia.com

Seraglia couture uses antique, old, reclaimed, and unexpected materials to create lasting heirloom pieces. They will work to commission individual pieces, and will include your own items, stones, or metals if desired.

Stephen Einhorn   http://www.stepheneinhorn.co.uk

An ethically responsible company that only uses manufacturers and materials that are eco-friendly and socially responsible

Verde Rocks!   http://gwen-davis.com

A completely sustainable jewelry line using only the most natural and organic materials such as rare Timber Bamboo, rare unused vintage beads, and antique Swarovski crystals

Coco's Shoppe   http://cocosshoppe.com

Synthetic Diamonds

Diamond Nexus   http://www.DiamondNexusLabs.com

White Sapphire   http://www.TheNaturalSapphireCompany.com

Cubic Zirconia   http://www.czfantasy.com

Russian Diamonds   http://www.russianbrilliants.net

chapter 3

wedding attire

The Bride's Gown

Good taste and classic, timeless styling are a cornerstone of a good sustainable approach to living. Remember this when you choose the attire for yourself and everyone else in your wedding party. Nothing makes you feel more like the bride than the gown you will wear when you walk down the aisle. There are so many options and some unexpected alternatives available, from high-end to vintage. One thing is for certain, and that is that you can find the perfect dress for you—one that is a reflection or your style, taste, and values. Just give yourself some extra time before you plop down your money on the dress of your dreams. Use this time to learn more about how wedding attire is produced and how you can choose a dress that wasn't made by child labor or with environmentally harmful chemicals.

Despite its beauty and glamour, the fashion industry is currently one of the largest pollutants and also uses more child labor and sweatshop labor than any other industry. In the U.S., 13 million acres of cotton is grown each year—most of which is grown using large amounts of potentially harmful pesticides and insecticides. (Source: The Pesticide Action Network-PAN)

Better alternatives are becoming more available, such as organic cotton, which is grown without the use of synthetic chemical fertilizers, pesticides, growth regulators, or defoliants. There are some high-end designers who are now producing fashion using sustainable materials and refusing to use sweatshop labor. Silk, hemp, bamboo, or even organic cotton are materials that have graced some of the runway shows from Paris to Milan to New York. The ultimate bridal fashionista—Vera Wang— has incorporated some green and fair-trade pieces into her collection, and London-based Jessica Ogden makes vintage fashion from recycled clothing. To encourage more designers to become more sustainable, a new site just launched that provides information about creating high-style eco design, ecodesignlab.com. This program also works with developing nations to create positive connections, training, and relationships between them and larger nations. Another site, stylewillsaveus.com, also promotes eco-chic design.

Sustainable Fabric

Abaca Derived from a variety of the banana plant. The fibers that come from its stalk are removed to make rope and then to weave fabric.

Bamboo One of the most widely used, completely sustainable, natural resources in the world. It is naturally resistant to all bacteria and microbes. No pesticides or chemicals are needed to grow it, and it has its own anti-bacterial properties so it does not need to be treated with harmful chemicals. Bamboo is use for food, shelter, fuel, fabric, and clothing.

Cashmere One of the most precious fabrics available, and it supports many smaller developing countries. It is a renewable and sustainable fabric.

Designer Surplus is the leftover fabrics from another designer's creations. Designers use these fabrics to create new pieces while reducing waste and consuming less.

Hemp Hemp fiber is one of the strongest and most durable of all natural textile fibers. Less land is needed for growing hemp crops since it is such a fast-growing product. It's also a very hearty crop and doesn't require the use of pesticides or other chemical aids to ensure a large yield. Hemp is one of the most sustainable fabric resources available.

Linen Also a natural produced fabric, it is derived from the flax plant. Must be grown organically for it to be truly sustainable, and it is often a pricey option. But it is extremely durable and is a great summertime fabric.

Lyocell A sustainable fiber and eco-friendly alternative to cotton that is made from wood pulp harvested from tree farms. The production process for Lyocell is very friendly to the environment friendly and is 100% biodegradable.

Recycled and Vintage With classic styling, what's old is new again and again.

Organic Cotton Traditional cotton farming is one of the most environmentally destructive agricultural activities. The amount of chemicals used to manufacture just one article of cotton clothing has a significant effect on the land, air, water, and people living in cotton-production areas. Organic cotton is produced at a slightly greater cost, but it is produced in a sustainable way. As more consumers choose organic cotton, the demand will drive the price down. So choose organic cotton!

Silk A very eco-friendly textile. Silk is still produced in a traditional fashion, is a renewable resource, and is biodegradable. Throughout time, silk has long been a precious product for many areas of the world, and is still a key component to their economic success.

Tencel A synthetic product, it is sustainably manufactured from wood pulp. It is a good example of how companies can manufacture textiles in a sustainable way and by using renewable resources. Tencel is made via a non-toxic, chemical-free process, and its by-products can be used in other industries.

Twill Woven from cotton, must be designated as organic to be sustainable. Another very good warm-weather fabric choice.

Ingeo A fabric woven from corn, it can have a luxurious almost silk-like finish.

Bridesmaid Dresses

Before you choose the dresses your dear wedding party will wear, take a trip down to your local thrift shop and you're sure to find at least a few discarded bridesmaid dresses. Sometimes you might even find a veritable bridesmaid dress extravaganza. Sadly, bridesmaids often spend upwards of $200 for a dress they will never wear again. And then there are the shoes. Now there are great alternatives to the same boring bridesmaid dress, and many creative ways to create a unifying look. Don't add to the waste by forcing your friends to spend money on something they will only wear (grudgingly) one time in their lives. And who buys those used bridesmaid dresses at the thrift stores anyway?

The Groom and His Men

There's nothing wrong with a nice, well-cut suit as an alternative to the typical tuxedo. My husband bought a new dark navy suit to wear to our daytime wedding, and he looked dashing (in my humble opinion). There also seems to be a trend to have all of the groomsmen wear matching jackets, ties, belts, pants, which can make them look like they're on their way to a frat party, not a wedding. Since it's unlikely that you are going to appeal to everyone's taste at the same time, chances are good that some of the guys will only wear these once, like the ill-fated bridesmaid dresses. Just bear this in mind, and consider letting everyone wear their own suits in similar shades of grey, blue, or black. If you must, perhaps you can have a necktie, bowtie, or cummerbund set made out of sustainable materials. At the very least, use good taste to dress the guys, and they'll get more than one day out of their outfits!

Flower Girls and Ring Bearers

When I was planning my wedding, one of the hardest things was try-ing to decide what the little ones should wear. I found that most wed-ding attire looks like a first communion dress, or something that would make a kid so uncomfortable they might not make it down the aisle at all. For some unknown reason, the options for flower girls and ring bearers are pretty limited. Luckily, there are plenty of non-wed-ding specific dresses out there that can easily be used for a wedding. You just have to be a little creative and not want to have your wed-ding look exactly like every other wedding out there. Sounds pretty good, doesn't it?

Make a Better Choice

When you select the attire for your wedding day, think about the impact the choice you make will have. And avoid clothing that is made in unhealthy, unsafe working conditions. According to the World Health Organization, 20,000 people die each year in develop-ing countries as a result of the chemicals sprayed on non-organic cot-ton. U.S. farm workers suffer from approximately 300,000 pesticide related illnesses each year. Five of the top nine chemicals used on cot-ton in the U.S. are known cancer-causing agents. A problem both in the U.S. and abroad, consumers can really help make a difference. Just refuse to buy anything that was produced by a "sweatshop." You can get more information at different websites like organic cottonplus.com, infomat.com (fashion industry information and search engine), earthspeaks.com, and atoexpo.com (all things organic). Believe me, if you saw some of the places where wedding clothes are made, the pretty white dresses dancing around the bridal magazines would really start to look pretty drab. So keep the spirit of your wedding joyful, and don't add to the sorrow of other less fortunate people.

Reduce

- **Say No to White:** Get a dress in your best color and truly dazzle with your unique flare. Did you know that those super-white wedding dresses got that way from a toxic chemical process? Opt for not-quite-white and get a wedding dress made from non-chemically treated, natural, earth-friendly fabric; soy, hemp silk, organic silk, organic cotton, organic wool, tencel, and bamboo are the main fabrics available.
- **Support Fair Trade:** Purchase your gown from a company that practices fair trade. (Fair Trade practices include: good wages for workers, adequate employee benefits like healthy work environments, fair hours, and health care.)
- **Keep it Simple:** Get a simple dress and add the pretty details yourself.
- **Buy Local:** Support a local designer or dressmaker in your area, and there will be little or no cost from transporting the garment from overseas. (Plus, you'll be feeding money back into the local environment, which is a main tenet of eco-consumerism.) Look into local design programs—you might be able to find a student who will create your gown for you at a mere fraction of the price you would pay for a retail dress. You can be sure that no one else will walk down the aisle wearing the same thing as you.

- **Don't Buy Sweatshop:** You can do research online at sites like sweatshopwatch.org or consumerreports.org to see if your designer has sound business practices.
- **Spend Less:** Keep the amount you spend on your dress to a minimum, and you can reallocate your funds elsewhere, like toward a down payment on a house!
- **Look for Sustainable Fabric:** Look into finding a dress made from sustainable fabric—such as hemp silk, hemp cotton, organic cotton, organic silk, linen, soy, or tencel. These fabrics are becoming more available and many top designers are integrating them into their looks—Oscar de la Renta has even fashioned a couture dress out of hemp silk and sent it down the runway.
- **Support a Charity:** Do more than just reduce your impact, and buy something to spice up your wedding duds with cotton flowers made in conjunction with Citta and women in Nepal, who use the money to provide health care and education programs for their community (citta.org).
- **Be Creative:** Turn your bridesmaids into walking décor by having them carry pretty parasols or paper fans with flower motifs, and then they can all wear their own dresses in matching colors.
- **Ask the Right Questions:** If the guys do wear rented tuxes, look into the dry cleaning and storage practice of the rental company—is it healthy? Do they use toxins that are harmful to humans and to the environment? Ask the question, and perhaps you can inspire a change if it has not taken place yet.

Reuse

- **Wear Your Mother's Dress:** Can you wear your mother's dress? Or maybe your grandmother, aunt, cousin, or friend would welcome sharing their own gown with you for your special day.

- **Share Your Dress:** Pick a dress with a friend, sister, or cousin who is also getting married and make a pact to share the dress between the two of you. This will give even more meaning to the dress because it will hold such special memories for both of you.

- **Borrow Something:** Wear accessories lent to you by family or friends, rather than purchasing new items. This will also take care of the "something borrowed."

- **Use Earth-Friendly Dry Cleaning:** It's better for your dress and better for the environment. Don't wrap it in plastic—the chemicals from the plastic could ruin your dress. Put it in a box (with no window) wrapped in non-dyed paper. Store it in a mild, dry climate—a cedar closet would be ideal. You will ensure someone, someday can wear your dress on their wedding day.

- **Get Your Gown at a Trunk Show:** Trunk shows tend to be where designers sell their sample dresses—dresses they've used in runway shows, advertising shoots, and other events. Dress sizes can vary, based on whether it went down the runway or not. Though you may need to do slight alterations, you can find some pretty amazing items this way.

- **Don't Buy Any One-Time-Use Items:** Don't get the typical bridal shoes that you'll only wear once—get a pair of strappy sandals, or simple flats, then dress them up with ribbons or flowers (fabric flowers—they don't get crushed on the dance floor). Bags, wraps, shoes, and any other accessories for the bride and the bridesmaids should also be able to be re-worn again and again.

- **Avoid the Look-Alike Look:** Ask yourself, do you really need to have all of your bridesmaids dressed in the same exact dress? Or can you simply choose a style and a color palette and let the girls get dresses that suit them better? You can have them all wear the same wrap, shawl, jewelry, or flowers so there is a degree of symmetry for the photographs. Think of this as a way of warding off the proliferation of waste that fills our landfills. Suits, shirts, and ties worn by the groomsmen should also be things they will wear again after the wedding.

- **Avoid Throw-Away Flower Girl Dresses:** Spruce up a simple dress that can be worn again with a sassy sash (you can even make the sash yourself). Add ruffled collars, strategically placed bows, an organza overlay, or a tulle underskirt; your flower girl dresses will be one of a kind, and the girls will have dresses they can wear for every day.

- **Customize with Details:** Turn your girls into real flower girls by temporarily sewing paper or fabric flowers all over a simple sundress. After the wedding they'll have something they can keep, with or without the flowers. Fabric appliqués are another great way to customize a plain dress and turn it into a one-of-a-kind creation that your girls will be thrilled to wear again.

- **Let the Men Wear Their Own Suits:** The men can wear their own dark-colored suits, with their own ties. Whenever my husband wears his suit and tie from the wedding, I think of our special day!

- **Unify With Matching Ties:** As for your men—yes, you can have them rent tuxedoes, if this is what you want. Or you can have them wear their own black, blue, or khaki suits—unify the look with matching ties, boutonnieres, or cummerbunds.

Recycle

- **Think Ahead:** Get a dress that can be remade into a fun, flirty cocktail dress post-wedding.
- **Help Someone Else:** Donate your dress to a charitable organization and help make someone else's wedding dreams come true.
- **Invest in Recyclable Materials:** Natural fabric that hasn't been dyed or treated with toxic chemicals is not only healthier for you, but it is more beautiful and richer feeling than chemically altered material. You can also be sure it will be recycled someday rather than seeping chemicals back into the earth in a landfill.

something old, something new

When Sarah Walsh Esposito was married in 2004, she wore a beautiful dress that was truly one of a kind. The first time she saw the dress was at a the New York bridal atelier of Mark Ingram. The dress was dazzling—and the price was equally blinding. At $5500, Sarah just wasn't sure that this was indeed the dress for her. A little while later, Sarah went back to the atelier with her mother—this time for a wedding dress sample sale. Women were grabbing dresses left and right in the small space, but in the midst of the frenzy Sarah managed to secure an Angel Sanchez dress for just $1500. She then went to a seamstress who fit the dress to her frame perfectly, adding some lace from her mother's wedding dress to the bodice. Sarah looked stunning in her unique gown, and she couldn't have been happier.

Eco-Chic Resources:
Fashion

Though eco-fashion is still in the early stages, using a little creativity, you can find the good sustainable fashion options you desire—even for your own bridal gown. The following is a list of designers and resources to help:

Apparel

Swati Argade   http://swatiargade.com
Her dresses are so beautiful they could easily be worn by bridesmaids, or even as a unique bridal gown.

The Dressmarket   http://www.thedressmarket.net
Used and some samples are available; they have a pretty good selection

Emer Maher Dowling   http://emermaherdowling.com
Lovely eco-chic items that are definitely not your typical wedding fare

Boll Organic   http://bollorganic.com
Organic cotton men's shirts

The Glass Slipper Project   http://glassslipperproject.org
If you donate your dress to them, it will go to a high school senior who can't afford to buy a dress for her prom.

Annatarian   http://annatarian.com

Hip California design company that makes eco-bridal wear

The Bridal Garden   http://bridalgarden.org

Sells designer dresses at a deep discount to benefit Sheltering Arms Children's Services

Making Memories Breast Cancer Foundation

http://makingmemories.org

Gently worn designer dresses; sales benefit breast cancer foundation (brides against breast cancer)

Conscious Clothing   http://getconscious.com

Stylish hemp/silk wedding gowns and bridesmaid dresses; each dress is cut and sewn to order, with attention to detail

AFESIP Fair Fashion   http://afesip.org

Asian-inspired clothing; lovely creative alternatives for bridesmaid dresses, or even wedding gowns. This organization combats trafficking of women and children for sex slavery in southeast Asia.

Loomstate   http://loomstate.org

Accessories

Colette Malouf   http://colettemalouf.com

Beautiful ideas and designs if you want to be a little different

Bon Bon Oiseau   http://bonbonoiseau.com

Bonbon's famous handcrafted feather, leather, and chain corsages and tiny hair adornments can transform your bridal apparel into dazzling pieces.

B Jewelry   http://bjewelry.net

Hair clips with flower adornments, bridesmaid jewelry

Madame Fancy Pants   http://madamefancypants.com

Beautiful jewelry made from found items

Rose Flash   http://roseflash.ca

Fabric and Trim

Sustainable Cotton   http://sustainablecotton.org

Has resources and information about why you should buy organic cotton, and where you can get organic cotton products

Aurora Silk   http://aurorasilk.com

Sells silk fabric, organic cotton fabric, hemp fabric, and rayon in case you choose to have a designer make your dress for you. You can request fabric samples before you place a larger order.

Repro Depot   http://reprodepot.com

Appliqué and fabric to spiff up a dress and make it wedding-worthy

Hemp Traders	http://hemptraders.com
Ingeo Fibers	http://www.ingeofibers.com
Jasco Fabrics	http://jascofabrics.com
NUI Organics	http://nuiorganics.com
The Hemp Store	http://www.thehempstore.co.uk

chapter 4

wedding registry

Many of your friends and family will want to send you engagement gifts, even if you don't have an engagement party. So start a registry earlier than later so that you do not end up with items you don't want, won't use, and can't return. At least 80 percent of you will register for gifts, and your guests will spend $19 billion on your gifts. Hence, your registry may technically have nothing to do with the actual wedding event, but it is a very integral part of the experience. The registry symbolizes your united future with your partner. It is one of the ways you both (ideally) get to decide what that future will actually look like. What is your style? Are you formal, casual, or somewhere in between?

Whatever you decide to do, the easiest and fastest way to register is online—at this point it's pretty much the norm. If you sign up on the TheKnot.com, you can list whatever retailers you wish all on one page whether or not they are affiliated with TheKnot. Even if you decide to make donations in lieu of gifts, you can still put that info on your very own "wedding home page" on TheKnot.

Take stock of what you need. In addition, there are a lot of recommended registry lists available, but if you're like me, you might already have a lot of the basic items. It's a good idea to take an inventory of everything you own, from kitchen, to bath, to bed. Are there big furniture items you would like? Some sites, like Crate and Barrel, have a "group gift" registry option. You can put something as big as a bed or a sofa, and your loved ones can pitch in for that particular selection. But bear in mind, most people prefer to give you their own individual gift.

The amount of products purchased in conjunction with all of the weddings taking place each year has resulted in practically every retail business offering some sort of wedding registry option. Retailers as diverse as Home Depot and Chase, Target, and adventure outfitter REI have wedding registries. With so much money being spent on your behalf, just think of what an enormous difference you and everyone else can make by selecting items that are eco-chic—such as bamboo bowls, items made from recycled glass and organic fabrics, and even products whose profits go directly back to support the local economies that produced them. Or, you might take generosity to another level by having your guests make a donation to the Oxfam Unwrapped Wedding List, or purchase your gifts via idofoundation.org, where your retailers—Target, Home Depot, and others—donate a portion of the gift price to your selected charity. You might decide to do a combination of traditional gifts and a donation.

How do you know if you should support a particular company as you register? What I do is to identify companies according to what business practices they are adopting and if they are making an effort to effect positive change in the world. Some of this information is available in the resources section of this book and other information might be found with a little searching on the Web. A great consumer information site run by the U.S. government is consumeraction.gov. A growing number of sites have really cool products that are good for you and everyone else, such as treehugger.com, idealbite.com, and goodsthatgive.com. And even a company such as Crate and Barrel, which may not necessarily be top of mind for eco-consciousness, is beginning to embrace the greener way of doing things. Did you know that they have developed an entire product line from bamboo wood, a highly sustainable resource? Now—get busy shopping!

Reduce

- **Eliminate Extra Packaging:** Have retailers hold your items until after the wedding. This will allow you to make changes once the whirlwind of the wedding is over. And, if you decide to return items, you won't waste packaging materials.
- **Support Companies Doing Good:** Register with companies that are striving to embrace sustainable and fair trade practices (where are the goods being produced, what environmental standards does it follow).
- **Choose Sustainable Materials:** Select items made from sustainable materials (bamboo, reclaimed wood, organic cotton, hemp). Walnut, oak, birch and pine are among a number of readily available, sustainable timbers.
- **Buy Local:** Support local artisans and craftsmen, both here and abroad, by registering for their items.

- **Get Only What You Need:** Consider registering for one set of dishes—either a china pattern that can be used every day or an everyday that can be used for more formal occasions. Get universal wine glasses instead of white/red/port/etc. The recommended glassware/barware on most registry lists from wedding experts is ridiculous—whoever actually uses a demitasse spoon? And do you really need margarita glasses? Or dessert wine glasses? Take it down a notch, and keep your glassware to a minimum . . . even the finest restaurants often use a universal wine glass for everything from wine to water. Don't necessarily go for the many different kitchen sets, since you may already have many items already. Only order what you need.

- **Reduce Junk Mail:** Once you open a registry, you may start getting more direct mail. You can remove your name from direct marketers' lists by going to the Direct Marketing Association website (http://www.dmaconsumers.org).

- **Get Non-Toxic Goods:** Some health risks may be associated with Teflon, so you may wish you go for something with less controversy when it comes to your cookware. Stainless steel also has some issues, since it is really a mixture of several different metals, including nickel, chromium, and molybdenum, all of which can trickle into foods. Anodized aluminum cookware seems to be among the safer alternatives on the market (Calphalon and All Clad are examples of anodized aluminum cookware). Another good choice for cookware is cast iron, known for being durable and providing even heat distribution. Lodge Manufacturing is the leading American producer of cast-iron cookware.

- **Order Based on Your Lifestyle:** You don't have to order twelve (or thirteen) place settings for your china. You can just as easily order a set of six (or eight), but have your everyday china coordinate so that you can always use it to supplement for larger parties. You might also skip the teacups and saucers, since most people never even use them. Instead of dessert and salad plates, just go for the salad plate and use it interchangeably.

- **Take Care of Your Stuff:** Invest in items designed to take care of and protect your nice things—the knife sharpener, the silver chest, the plate protector.

Reuse

- **Keep it in the Family:** Add to heirlooms you might have, such as Grandma's china dinner plates; mix and match with other patterns to create a complete set.
- **Buy Quality:** Choose quality over trends; get classic, well-made items you will keep for many years. I have things in our kitchen that are more than thirty years old, such as cast iron pans and excellent chef's knives. When you buy quality and take good care of your things, they should last for a very long time.

Recycle

- **Buy Recycled Items:** Reclaimed wood furniture is now available through many different retailers, and this is one way to make use of resources. Super-chic retailers like ABC Carpet and Home sell—and advertise—their fabulous reclaimed wood furniture. Companies like Riverside Design Group make beautiful glass items, made from post-industrial/pre-consumer recycled glass, and each piece is made in the U.S.

- **Clean Out Your Closets:** Cleaning your closets, cupboards, and cabinets can make way for your new stuff. This is a perfect opportunity to recycle your items at thrift store or your local Salvation Army. As you sort through your things in preparation for the onslaught of wedding gifts, you may get rid of a lot of older items. If you do, look to specific companies, like IBM and Hewlett-Packard, who actually have "take-back" programs that effectively salvage some components, rather than fill more landfills.

- **Don't Fill the Landfills:** Recycle the paper and packaging associated with your presents (hopefully you will be able to reduce this by having retailers hold your presents). And if you register for any electronic items with batteries, look to see if they carry the RBRC logo (the Rechargeable Battery Recycling Corporation, which facilitates the collection of used rechargeable batteries collected in an industry-wide "take-back" program for recycling. RBRC then processes the batteries via a thermal recovery technology that reclaims metals such as nickel, iron, cadmium, lead, and cobalt, repurposing them for use in new batteries.

Eco-Chic Resources: <u>Wedding Registry</u>

Charitable Alternatives to Gifts

Be the Change	http://bethechange.org
I Do Foundation	http://www.idofoundation.org
Just Give	http://www.justgive.org

Online Registries

GreenSage   http://greensage.com

A wedding registry with gifts that are energy efficient, non-toxic, recycled, reclaimed, naturally resourced, and biodegradable

Global Exchange   http://gxonlionestore.org

Register for all things ethical

Satara   http://www.satara-inc.com

Specializes in organic and natural-fiber products for the home. They have an online gift registry, which you can list on your registry page on TheKnot.com along with all of your other registries.

Green Living   http://green-living.com

Earth-friendly and fair-trade items; they have an online registry

Greenfeet   http://www.greenfeet.com

Sustainable and eco-friendly products for the home, with an online registry

Wiliams-Sonoma   http://williams-sonoma.com

You can register for cookware that won't be harmful to you and your family (studies show some Teflon-coated pans pose a hazard). Brands to check out include Calphalon, All-Clad, and Le Creuset.

Gaiam   http://gaiam.com

Replacements, Ltd.   http://replacements.com

Gift Certificate Programs

Poppy Cotton   http://poppycotton.com

Poppy Cotton's vibrant pop art–era floral pieces for the home are handmade using vintage fabrics, including everything from napkins and silk kerchiefs to curtains and tablecloths. You can't register online, but you can request gift certificates from the store.

Green Glass   http://greenglass.org

Company that converts empty, discarded bottles into beautiful glassware. They do not have a registry, but you can request gift certificates from your friends and family.

3R Living   http://3rliving.com

A home decor and lifestyle store dedicated to the principles of reducing waste, reusing unwanted or discarded materials, and recycling. They do not have a registry, but you can request gift certificates in lieu of gifts.

Drop Soul   http://dropsoul.com

A store filled with sustainable and cruelty-free products. Your guests can purchase gift certificates for you.

chapter 5

wedding invitation

The wedding invitation has become one of the most complicated elements of the wedding. Everything from the wording, to
the design, to when they should be mailed is debated and discussed
in every wedding magazine, book, and tv show out there. Over the
last decade, the wedding industry cognoscenti have convinced us
that it is crucial to have a highly personalized, detail-oriented wedding, and that much time and effort should be spent creating the
masterpiece that is to be your wedding invitation. An unfortunate
trend in the wedding industry is the increase in paper used for the
invitations, such as the elaborate "wedding wardrobe" some stationers recommend, which might include ten different pieces for
one invitation. Even the once optional save-the-date card has
become a requirement. So, with this in mind, let's just take a step

back for a minute and ponder how this wedding invitation trend might impact the bigger picture.

Did you know that the average American uses almost 700 pounds of paper every year? And did you know that much of that paper has been processed with chlorine bleach, making it non-recyclable and, even worse, totally toxic for the environment? So, once that beautiful invitation leaves your loving hands, it passes a short life and ends up, with little or no ceremony, in a landfill. Along with everyone else's wedding invitation (about 350 million, to be precise).

The U.S. paper industry consumes 12,430 square miles of forest per year, and most of these forests are found in the southeastern part of the country. You might think this is okay, since many of these forests have been grown expressly to be harvested and made into paper and other wood-based products. The problem with this system is the destruction of biodiversity that results from the single-species wood plantations in this part of the country. Roughly 40 percent of what were once diverse native pine forests are now single-species pulp plantations, designed to maximize the amount of wood pulp produced for making paper. These single-species forests have up to 95 percent lower biodiversity than indigenous forests. This results in natural erosions and an overall upset of the natural balance of everything from plants to insects, to air quality. Because most of these forests are on private land, there is very little the federal agencies can do about it. (Source: Forest Stewardship Council, fcus.org)

Luckily, tree-free and chlorine-free papers are carving a larger and larger niche out of the paper market, and large retailers like Staples are making pledges to seek out more earth-sensitive options. You can help grow this healthier segment of the industry when you choose the paper you will use for your wedding invitation. You shouldn't feel required to do anything, because there are a myriad of options available to you, all of which are perfectly acceptable in whatever circles you may travel in. In fact, the European trend is to limit the amount of paper to such a degree that many couples are sending a postcard invitation and requesting an email reply. And who's to say this isn't perfectly fine etiquette, since Emily Post isn't around for the Internet and thus can't weigh in on the subject.

Certainly, with all of the wedding invites going out every day, brides are among some of the paper industry's most important customers. So imagine that all of the brides started requesting recycled, recyclable papers, and maybe even began to simplify the design of the invitations as well. It stands to reason that the paper manufacturers might respond by producing more sustainable paper in order to service this market, don't you think?

Reduce

- **Go Digital:** Be ultra-modern and forgo printed invites altogether—send evites. You might even have a friend (or maybe you know digital design) to create an electronic piece of art for you. This also makes following up so much easier.
- **Be Early:** Send your wedding invitations earlier than planned so that you don't have to send a save-the-date card.
- **Simplify:** A very old-fashioned way of doing the wedding invitation would include up to fifteen pieces in the "wedding invitation wardrobe." Be a more modern bride and just have the invite with envelope and a smaller response card with an envelope, or follow the European trend and just have a simple postcard, with a telephone number or email address for all RSVPs.
- **Use Handmade Paper:** Reduce your impact on the environment by choosing handmade paper; no trees will be cut down

for the invitations, you'll be supporting the paper-making craft and the artisans who make your invitations.

• **Don't Invite the World:** Make one guest list and stick to it; don't have a "B" list of invitees. If you have a lower number of guests, enjoy your reduced costs (we put the extra money in the bank). Minimize your guest list, don't feel obligated to invite everyone you know. When you are first engaged, let people know "we are going to have something relatively small, mostly family." This will help you avoid hurting the feelings of your co-worker down the hall (for some reason, everyone loves to be invited to a wedding, even if they barely know the person).

• **Ask a Friend to Help:** Another way to reduce your impact and your cost is to ask a talented friend to design your invitation for you, and you can be sure your paper is eco-chic.

Reuse

• **Send Something Special:** Make your invitation a keepsake for your guests rather than something they will simply throw away; include an inspirational quote or a poem, or incorporate a theme into the invitation, such as spring. Make tulip-seed packets as your invitation, and attach smaller printed tags to the packet with your details; your friends and loved ones can plant the flowers to remind them of your special day with each colorful bloom. Make your invitation into a crossword puzzle with words meaningful to you. Or make paper or fabric flower invitations, send in a pretty little box, and your guests will be able to pin or sew the blossoms onto a bag, hat, blouse, or jacket.

• **Make Use of Leftover Paper:** Ask for any extra paper from the printer leftover from your invitations; use this to get crafty making thank-you notes after the wedding.

Recycle

- **Buy Recycled Paper:** Choose recycled- and recyclable-paper for invitations, response cards (if you use them), and thank-you notes, but check to see how much of the paper is made from post-consumer waste; the higher the percentage of recycled paper fibers, especially post-consumer, the better. Try making your own invitations with recycled, recyclable paper. There are a number of great companies that will even give you an easy-to-use design program that will make producing your own invites a snap. Or find clip art online or in a magazine to create your unique design.
- **Don't Use Adhesive Stamps:** Choose traditional moisten-and-stick postage stamps, if you can find them, in sheets or cardstock booklets. The self-adhesive stamps come with non-recyclable plastic sheet backing, which makes them less desirable.
- **Check the Postage:** Bring your invitations and response cards to the post office and have them weighed before you put postage on. You'll avoid unnecessary waste—and hassles—if you put the correct postage on before you attempt to mail the invites.
- **Encourage Recycling:** Include a "please recycle" note on your invitations as a reminder to your guests.
- **Avoid Filling the Landfills:** When you're done making your invites, recycle your printer cartridges. More than 300 million inkjet cartridges end up in American landfills every year. Many companies out there will take your used cartridges so they can re-ink them and resell them; Staples even gives you a discount when you bring them into the store.

Eco-Chic Resources:
Wedding Invitations

Do It Yourself

Invitesite   http://invitesite.com

You can customize the invitations further to make them truly one of a kind. Because you are handling the printing and the assembly, you choose the paper, and even better—these custom invitations are affordably priced.

Paporganics   http://paporganics.com

Sustainable stationery and gift wrap

Klee Paper   http://kleepaper.com

Seal-n-Send Invitations   http://www.seal-n-send.com

Sidepony   http://sidepony.com

Greg Barber Co.   http://gregbarberco.com

Eco Paper Co.   http://ecopaperco.com.au

Green Field Paper Co.   http://greenfieldpaper.com

Tree-Free Paper   http://rainforestweb.org

Stationers

Joy by Mel Lim   http://joybymellim.com
   Eco-conscious paper products

Twisted Limb Paper Works   http://twistedlimbpaper.com
   Handmade 100%-recycled invitations

Baglady Designs   http://baglady-designs.com

Oblation Papers and Press   http://oblationpapers.com

Sidepony   http://sidepony.com

Recycling Printer Cartridges

We Buy Empties   http://webuyempties.com

Inkjet Cartridge   http://inkjetcartridge.com

The eCycle Group   http://ecyclegroup.com

Inkjetman   http://inkjetman.com

Learn More About the Paper Industry

Forest Stewardship Council   http://fscus.org
   Current trends and information about what is happening with
   the world's forests and the impact of paper production

Rainforest Action Network   http://ran.org
   For information about paper and sustainability

Rainforest Alliance	http://www.rainforest-alliance.org
iRethink	http://irethink.com
Funding Factory	http://fundingfactory.com
The Dogwood Alliance	http://dogwoodalliance.org
Forest Ethics	http://forestethics.org
Natural Resources Defense Council	http://nrdc.org

chapter 6

flowers, style, and design

Depending on the location, much of the style and design of your wedding location will dictate how you will add your own style touch to the décor. The location I used for my wedding was pleasant and simple, with big open windows that featured a beautiful vista of fall colors, so I didn't need to do much to make it pretty. More than likely, you will choose flowers or perhaps other design elements to communicate your particular theme and vision. You might stick to centerpieces, some sort of alter or chuppah décor, or perhaps the entrance to the place (or places, if you do not have the ceremony and reception at one location). As for other areas, such as the bridal suite (if there is one), rest rooms, bar area, or place card table, you might feel that you want to add your special touch in these spots too.

Wedding flowers are the lion's share of any florist's yearly revenue, and flowers also have a significant environmental and social impact on the world. Your selection of what flowers to use will indeed make an impact—positive or negative—on the environment. You may not realize this, but the toxic chemicals used on flower farms in Central and South America poison groundwater and the soil. These chemicals become a part of the food chain when birds eat the sprayed plants, and then when they migrate, these birds spread the chemicals globally. So, every flower counts and as more people choose organic flowers, the

Working with a Florist

- Confirm exactly what flowers you want and don't want for the wedding; some suggestions: bridal bouquet, bridesmaid bouquets, nosegay for the mothers, boutonnières for the groom, groomsmen, ushers, and father's centerpieces, entrance (for reception and ceremony), restroom/s, additional wedding party rooms
- Find out if they ever work with organic and/or sustainable growth flowers/farms
- Will they tell you who their flower suppliers are; can they source locally
- Are they willing to pick up and donate leftover flowers to charities for minimum fee
- Can you use your own vessels (vases/bowls)
- Ask them not to use the green gardeners foam, as this can not be recycled
- Let them know you would like to be able to eliminate any unnecessary waste from your arrangements; using floral wire and other devices render the arrangements unable to be composted, so keep things simple

market shift will cause farmers to convert their practices to using more sustainable methods.

You may not know how toxic and harmful common pesticides are, but a recent study from the National Cancer Institute shows a direct link with multiple cases of non-Hodgkin's lymphoma in farm workers. Pesticides like the commonly used Roundup contain other ingredients that can cause nausea, diarrhea, chemical pneumonia, laryngitis, and severe headaches. The small doses we use every day on our own lawns dissipates (into the atmosphere), so we probably are not exposed to harmful levels ourselves. But, the thousands of low-wage workers who harvest and package the flowers we use in the U.S.—more than half of all cut flowers sold in the U.S. are imported—are negatively affected by the use of unsafe pesticides. It may surprise you that, because flowers are not ingested, the U.S. Department of Agriculture doesn't regulate pesticide levels on them as imports. As a result, cut flowers are one of the world's most pesticide-intensive crops, and to ensure they have pretty flowers that live as long as possible, flower importers don't skimp on the amount of pesticide they use. In Ecuador, 60 percent of workers report that they have chronic headaches, nausea, blurred vision, and fatigue. (Source: http://laborrights.org, Fairness In Flowers, May 2006)

The good news is that you can find organic alternatives readily available. The fabulous organicbouquet.com ships some of the prettiest flowers that I have ever seen, and they're healthier and better for you, so you can feel free to enjoy their fragrance. They also work with brides to do wedding flowers. If you go this route, you will need to use whatever flowers are in season when you decide to get married. You can go with the online option, or you could seek out local farmers (go through the chamber of commerce) to purchase in-season flowers. A good online resource is localharvest.org;

Flowers by Season

Spring	Summer
Allium	Allium
Anemone	Amaryllis
Apple Blossoms	Aster
Billy Buttons	Bells of Ireland
Celosia	Billy Buttons
Cherry Blossoms	Calla Lily
Daffodils	Celosia
Dogwood	Dahlia (Late Summer)
Freesia	Delphinium
Iris	Fuchsia
Liatris	Geranium
Lilacs	Gladiola
Lily of the Valley	Honeysuckle
Lisianthus	Hydrangea
Narcissus	Liatris
Peony	Lisianthus
Ranunculus	Orange blossom
Quince	Peonies
Snapdragon	Pincushion
Sweet Pea	Queen Anne's Lace
Tulip	Roses
Violet	Saponaria
Waxflower	Snapdragon
	Speedwell
	Sunflower
	Tuberose
	Zinnia

Fall

- Amaryllis
- Anemones
- Aster
- Bittersweet
- Calla Lily
- Celosia
- Chinese Lantern
- Chrysanthemum
- Cock's Comb
- Dahlia
- Delphimium
- Fuchsia
- Hydrangea
- Liatris
- Lisianthus
- Narcissus
- Marigold
- Montbretia
- Protea
- Snapdragon
- Star of
  Bethlehem
- Sunflowers
- Tuberose
- Zinnia

Winter

- Amaryllis
- Daffodil
- Darnellia
- Ginestra
- Hyacinth
- Mimosa
- Paperwhite
  narcissus
- Star of
  Bethlehem
- Tulip

Year-Round

- Alstromeria
- Aster
- Baby's Breath
- Bachelor button
- Bird of Paradise
- Bouvardia
- Calla Lily
- Carnation
- Daisy
- Delphinium
- Eucalyptus
- Fern
- Freesia
- Gardenia
- Gerbera Gladiolus
- Iris
- Ivy
- Lily
- Orchid
- Rose
- Statice
- Stephanotis

they maintain a nationwide directory of local farms. Otherwise, you can find a traditional florist in your area who is willing to work with you to feature organic blooms. Again, you will need to make your selection based on seasonal availability, but a talented florist should be able to create something splendid no matter what time of year it is.

You might also consider alternatives to flowers such as votive candles, dried leaves, paper flowers, branches, evergreens, topiaries, plants, or even cake plates with prettily decorated cupcakes at each table. Or consider wedding favors wrapped in gorgeous paper with colorful ribbons piled ornamentally in the table center for a dual-purpose centerpiece. However you decide to decorate, consider what will become of the arrangement, the candles, or whatever other elements you may have once the wedding ends. Can you donate, give as gifts, or save the votives for your own use? It is such a terrible waste when such a beautiful thing is simply tossed away, so please make sure this isn't what happens on your wedding day.

Reduce

- **Go With Organic:** Lessen your environmental impact by using organically grown local flowers that are in season—they won't need much transportation to get to you, so you will reduce fuel costs.
- **Make Dual-Purpose Decor:** Create fabric-flower placecards or make paper leaves at each place setting, with each guest's name. You can include a safety pin so that your guests can wear your handmade creations after the wedding.
- **Light Some Candles:** Save money, and leftover waste, by using candles instead of flowers—the look can be even more striking,

especially for an evening event. Go for unscented, soy-based candles, and make sure you know the burn time (how long the candle will burn until it goes out). Try flower-shaped candles or pretty boxes shaped like flowers. Put one pillar candle in a glass hurricane for a simple centerpiece on each table. Place fruit, dried berries, or even autumn leaves around the hurricane for extra effect. Place colored pillar candles in tall glass votives with flower petals, pinecones, ivy, or even leaves lining the bottom of the vase.

- **Feature an Edible Arrangement:** Instead of flowers, use locally grown seasonal fruit in bowls on each table. Put little cakes or an assortment of cupcakes decorated with sugar flowers (organic) at each table as a centerpiece, in lieu of fresh flowers. Having a winter wedding? Ask your grandparents to send you (organic) oranges and/or lemons from balmy Florida, place bunches in ceramic footed bowls, and soon you will have a bright and cheery wedding reception.

- **Simplify:** Reduce the amount of flowers by floating a few blossoms in shallow vessels; dinner plate dahlias (late Summer or early Fall) or other wide-blooming flowers should do the trick. A table arrangement using a bunch of smaller vases featuring single blossoms in each vessel can be quite beautiful too.

- **Don't Use Balloons:** There are no earth-friendly balloons, no matter how you look at it. Balloons are dangerous to animals, who often eat them. Balloons are responsible for the deaths of thousands of sea turtles, dolphins, fish, and seabirds. Mass release of balloons is illegal in several U.S. states, including Connecticut, Florida, Tennessee, California, and Virginia, and similar legislation is pending in Massachusetts, Maryland, New York, and in some municipal locales. So skip the balloons, please.

- **Forgo Wedding-Themed Décor:** Don't waste your money and resources on overtly wedding-themed items for your décor—such as customized disposable cameras, one-time-use flower vases, canopies, or even wedding favors. Be creative, and be selective about how you add style to your event. Can the table signs be saved and made into something special after the wedding? Hold on to the crafty elements, ribbons, papers, and fabric, so that you can either keep them for your own post-wedding creations or give them to a creative friend to use.

- **Use Branches in Creative and Dramatic Ways:** Vibrant fall colors on branches can replace flower arrangements; hang votive candles, paper flowers, or even silver holiday ornaments on branches for dramatic effect.

- **Use Seasonal Items:** Ivy is a wonderfully fresh, festive, and readily available decorating element—and you can do so many different things with it, including wreaths, bouquets, swags, and centerpieces. Pinecones and pumpkins can be quite a nice, even quirky way to bring the outdoors in.

- **Add Paper, Fabric, and Ribbons for Color:** Hang colorful paper lanterns from the ceiling instead of centerpieces. Colorful ribbons or fabric at each place setting can add color so that just a few blossoms in the center will suffice. Bright swathes of fabric used as table clothes, table runners, napkins, or draped across the ceiling are an inexpensive, simple way to bring dramatic effect to the space.

- **Create a Little Mood Lighting:** Make your centerpieces out of little lamps, or use candlesticks with colored lampshades as your fashion statement.

- **Let the Vases Add Drama and Color:** Use brightly colored ceramic and glass vases with a few plain white flowers for a dramatic contrast; in winter, you can try this with paper whites or stephanotis. Or, reverse this idea with white ceramic, glass, and milk glass vessels, with red winterberries, green ferns, or even lemongrass.

Reuse

- **Choose Reusable Decorations:** Ribbons, fabric, even table signs can be reused after the wedding (put someone in charge of gathering these items on your behalf once the event is over). Dried or fresh flower wreaths can adorn the tables (with a glass hurricane and candles set in the center), and guests can take the wreaths home. An unusual and readily available centerpiece is boxwood. An evergreen plant, boxwood can be shaped into a classic presentation (remember Edward Scissorhands?), and then, it can still be used in someone's yard for many years.
- **Donate Your Flowers:** Identify a friend or family member to bring your flowers to a nursing home or to a hospital (it's a tax deduction). At the very least, make sure your guests bring the flowers home with them.
- **Make a Mix-and-Match Arrangement:** Put some lovely porcelain tea cups to good use by arranging them on each table with a small flower placed in each cup. Guests can take them home, or you can save the teacups for your home.
- **Use Your Own Vessels:** Give your florist vessels, such as mason jars or jelly jars—items that you might be able to collect and reuse on your wedding day. Or perhaps you can make your own votives or vases. Save glass jars over time, remove the labels, and wrap with fabric or paper, or even use glass paint to decorate in your own unique, chic, and festive way.
- **Use Something Living:** Grow herbs in clay pots as a centerpiece

for each table; place table signs in the pot to create a pretty table setting (you can have a calligrapher make the signs beautiful for you to dress it up). Put individual potted plants or flowers on the table in a bunch, with a little sign encouraging your guests to take one home with them. Violets, zinnias, and even ferns would be lovely featured this way. Use flowering bulbs—amaryllis, narcissus, and hyacinth, which can go home with guests to be enjoyed in their own homes. Place them in tall, glass, cylindrical containers for a dramatic effect. Wheat grass is pretty and fresh enough looking that you could even use it to dress up your tables, and then you can eat it. Topiary is also a beautiful, vintage way to adorn your space, and these can go home with guests or can be donated to a nursing home for further enjoyment.

- **Feature Bouquet Centerpieces:** Make your bridal and bridesmaid bouquets do double duty as table centerpieces.

add a little light to the night

When Anne Chertoff and David Tavalin were married in June 2003, they decided they wanted to create a very special mood for the celebration. Both Anne and David are fans of classic romantic movies that feature Audrey Hepburn and Clark Gable. For the evening soiree, they asked their event designer to use several little lamps on each table to create an intimate setting. With the pretty lavender silk lampshades and the glowing light, Anne and David created a unique setting, reminiscent of a classic dining establishment that old Hollywood would have frequented. Also, they were able to reduce the amount of flowers needed for each centerpiece. This stylish, simple eco-chic solution added a special glow to the event.

Recycle

- **Use Recyclable Materials:** Be sure everything you use can either be recycled or composted—that means having organic flowers because they won't introduce toxic elements back into the environment. Make the design elements of your day out of items you can recycle (paper, ribbons, recyclable plastics). Be aware of the specific tools used to make your arrangements, such as non-recyclable floral tape and green foam. If you do have traditional floral arrangements (and hopefully they will be organic), at least ask the florist to keep them natural and simple so that you aren't creating any unnecessary waste.

Eco-Chic Resources:
Flowers, Style, and Design

Flowers

Organic Bouquet   http://www.organicbouquet.com
California Organic Flowers. Organic flowers and gifts. Shipped next day

PANNA (Pesticide Action Network
North America)   http://panna.org

Homeless Gardenc Project   http://homelessgardenproject.org

Manic Organics Flowers   http://www.manicorganicsflowers.com

Seabreeze Organic Farm   http://www.seabreezed.com

Local Harvest   http://www.localharvest.org

Candles

Cox and Cox   http://coxandcox.co.uk
Bird candles, clip-on butterflies, linen ribbon, and more

Greenspace Candles   http://greenspacecandles.com

Ribbon

Repro Depot   http://reprodepot.com
They specialize in vintage grosgrain ribbon patterns.

Custom Paper   http://custompaper.com
A variety of ribbon, including midori, organza, dupioni.

Paper and Fabric

Blume Box   http://blumebox.com

They sell pretty colored boxes that are a great cost-effective
way to add color and style to the flowers—boxes can be reused
or recycled.

Jude Miller   http://judemiller.com

Resource for handcrafted paper flowers

chapter 7

wedding favors

You may want to show a little gratitude to your wedding guests for sharing your special day with you by giving them a gift. Wedding favors have become so de riguer that they are almost expected. But more often than not, guests simply toss the gifts they receive right into the trash. This may be because brides and grooms sometimes think their guests would just love to have a frame engraved with their wedding date, or a clock, or a wine bottle, or anything else you can think of. It is difficult to find one item that will please everyone, but it is possible.

There's practically an entire "mini-industry" for wedding favors. Before we go any further, I would like to mention one thing—you do not have to give your guests a wedding favor. The event, the party, the music, the food, the company—all of these are your "favor" to the guests. Give them a nice time, and it is very likely that they won't even notice the absence of a favor—if they do, they might even thank you for it. There are other ways to "thank" your guests and to give them a feeling of joy—make a donation in their behalf. This might just mean more to them than a little trinket. For my wedding, we made a donation to the Habitat for Humanity. I made a little sign at the seating card table that read: "We have made this donation on behalf of our guests so that other people might have a brighter future too."

Another idea is to offset whatever environmental "footprint" your wedding may result in by giving your guests carbon credits as favors. Your footprint is however much energy you will consume by having your wedding. You can calculate your average emissions based on air and car travel and the CO_2 produced by other aspects of the wedding, then calculate the amount per person. You can purchase the "credits" from Native Energy. Native Energy, based in Vermont, will use the money you donate to them to support renewable energy projects, such as farm methane and wind energy, which aim to reduce global carbon emissions. Give each guest a certificate with an explanation of the project.

The wedding industry now reports that favors are getting bigger and more ostentatious. TheKnot.com includes favors as one of the hot trends for 2006, noting that "robust welcome bags are gaining attention," and some brides are even giving their guests two gifts, one at the beginning and one at the end of the event. I can only encourage you to use this as an opportunity to reduce your consumption and the post-event waste. You can do this by replacing the favor idea with a donation in your guests' honor. You can also reduce waste by giving your guests something they will like—and use—after the wedding.

Reduce

- **Don't Do Favors:** Make a donation and avoid throwaway items after the wedding.
- **Give Something Edible:** Cookies, or biscotti, or even little candies for the car ride home. Or fresh organic fruit to complement your delicious cake. You can make cookies and wrap them individually, or even hand out homemade preserves. If you have a country wedding, you could give each guest an individual jar of homemade barbecue sauce.
- **Keep Packaging to a Minimum:** Make the gift something cute and decorative, such as a pretty picture frame or colorful plant, and you won't need to use extra packaging to wrap the gifts.

Reuse

- **Make the Favor Serve a Dual Purpose:** Something with the guest's name, such as a nice placecard holder that can double as a picture frame for reuse after the wedding.
- **Make Your Flowers the Favor:** I think this is the best reusable favor idea—to give each person their own potted flowering plant, such as an African violet or even vibrantly green wheatgrass, to enjoy after the wedding. During the event, their gift is a part of the table decoration.
- **Find Another Use for Cookie Cutters:** Make your guests quirky little ornaments out of holiday-inspired tin cookie cutters—trees, stars, or even heart cookie cutters with either photos or decorative paper cut to the shape of the cutter and glued on one side with a ribbon.

Recycle

- **Give Something Recycled:** Many designers are creating fresh, chic recycled gifts—made out of everything from paper and cardboard to candy wrappers.
- **Give Something Recyclable:** Whatever you give, try to make sure that all pieces are recyclable and biodegradable.
- **Make Candles:** You can use old candles melted down, or use muffin tins, tart molds, or cookie cutters to make your guests special creations.

Eco-Chic Resources: <u>Wedding Favors</u>

Coffee, Tea and Treats

Inspired Brew   http://inspiredbrew.com

Sells tea through their "Charitea" program, which supports efforts to eliminate child labor in Bolivian mines. Give packets of tea for wedding favors.

June Taylor Organic Preserves   http://junetaylorjams.com

Purveyors of fine artisanal food, and they work with local family-owned farms

Good Harvest Market   http://goodharvestmarket.com

You can give the gift of health with an organic fruit basket for your wedding guests or for out-of-town guests in their hotel rooms. They can arrange gift baskets and boxes with any theme and price.

Green Mountain Coffee	http://greenmountaincoffee.com
The Republic of Tea	http://republicoftea.com
Dagoba Organic Chocolate	http://dagobachocolate.com
Rococo Chocolates	http://rococochocolates.com

Vintage, Craft, Reusable, and Fair-Trade Items

Pixel Girlshop   http://pixelgirlshop.com
Cute unique quirky items for favors, including notecards and vintage wallpaper magnets

Ex Libris Anonymous   http://bookjournals.com
Fun, repurposed journals for useful favors

Rising Tide   http://rtfairtrade.com
Fair-trade boutique

Taraluna Gifts   http://taraluna.com
Fair-trade, organic gifts, and products

The Enterprising Kitchen   http://theenterprisingkitchen.org
A non-profit social service enterprise that sells handmade soaps and candles while providing workforce training to those in need

Global Crafts   http://globalcrafts.org

Handmade gifts made by craftspeople in developing countries, providing them with income-generating opportunities

A Greater Gift   http://www.agreatergift.org

Favor ideas for under $10, including a wooden box from Tibet with pretty detailing. All items are produced by local communities, and follow fair-trade practices.

EcoParti   http://ecoparti.com

Global Exchange   http://globalexchange.org

Donations

American Diabetes Association   http://diabetes.org

Make a donation instead of giving out favors and you'll get a card from the foundations that you can give to your guests to let them know about the donation.

UNICEF   http://unicef.org

When you make a donation, they will provide you with tent cards that you can feature at your wedding.

CO2Balance   http://co2balance.com

Give your guests a real planted tree—actually, a certificate that says a tree was planted on their behalf.

The CarbonNeutral Company   http://www.carbonneutral.com

chapter 8

health and beauty

Like most brides, you're probably planning to get into the best shape of your life for your wedding day. I mean, if you were ever going to do it, now is the time, right? Well, you might have noticed that gyms, magazines, and other businesses are on to you—several times a year you can find a "Bridal Boot Camp" at the gym and an almost constant supply of magazine articles that target the bride looking to get buff for her big day. Getting healthy is an excellent goal and seems to be something both brides and grooms incorporate into their plans at this life-changing time. I am a big supporter of taking the necessary steps to become the best you can be. I recommend going for it—hire that trainer, get that nutritionist, and enjoy every day as you move closer and closer to that walk down the aisle and the new and improved you. When you've got your get-healthy program together, be sure to also take stock of the personal care products, cosmetics, and toiletries, that you use. Some of those items might be counterproductive to your goal of the healthy lifestyle.

You may be surprised to learn that many of the products and brands you trust contain harmful ingredients like benzene, a petroleum derivative in nail polish and blush that disrupts the endocrine system and causes hormonal imbalance. And other commonly found ingredients, phathalates and parabens, are both known causes of birth defects. And six types of parabens have been found in breast cancer tissue. (Source: *Journal of Applied Toxicology*, 2004) Many fragrances contain suspected carcinogens that are associated with cancer and can harm your organs and reproductive system. Kevin Donegan, spokesperson for the Breast Cancer Fund, has been reported as saying that, "unlike drugs, cosmetics do not undergo extensive testing before the FDA allows them on the market. New scientific research shows that sometimes low-dose exposures to toxic chemicals can be more harmful than high-dose exposures, contrary to conventional thinking that low-dosage exposure is not harmful. Our position is that chemicals linked to cancer and birth defects do not belong in cosmetics and body-care products, period." (Source: Breast Cancer Fund, 2006) Before you schedule your manicure and pedicure for the wedding day, choose the polish wisely—women in cities around the world, including Chicago, have recently raised awareness and concern over ingredients contained in popular nail polish brands like OPI. At issue are the toxic chemicals known or suspected to cause cancer, birth defects, and other serious health problems. More information can be found through the Campaign for Safe Cosmetics (http://safecosmetics.org). (Source: *Chicago Tribune*, Health Beat, Julie Deardorff, May 2, 2006)

Fortunately, there are companies with socially responsible product lines. For further information about the rising concern over the unhealthy ingredients used in common products, check out the Japan Offspring Fund which provides information in the form of a poster explaining the problems, dangers, and some choices to help you find safer products, or the website organicconsumers.org.

Reduce

- **Avoid Toxic Ingredients:** Some perfumes and other fragranced beauty products contain phthalates, which are suspected of causing cancer, birth defects, and irritation, and are present in many personal care products.
- **Try Hydrosols:** A hydrosol is the water that remains after using steam or water distillation to create an essential oil, which can be used as facial toners or in other skin-care products. It can also be used as a light cologne or body spray.
- **Find Non-Toxic Products:** There are a number of chemical-free beauty product alternatives. Some are in the form of essential oils, many of which have been used to trigger positive psychological and physical reactions. Aromas such as bergamot, grapefruit, jasmine, and lavender, for instance, all smell great and have also been reported to help reduce stress, while cypress and orange are supposed to support confidence. Organically grown essential oils are much healthier for the environment, the people who cultivate them, and the people who use them.
- **Support Companies Doing Good:** Choose products from companies like Burt's Bees (which is owned by Estée Lauder), Kiss My Face, and Avalon Organics. All of these companies

have signed the Compact for Safe Cosmetics, a pledge that their products are free of chemicals known or suspected of causing cancer, mutation, or birth defects.

- **Avoid Benzoyl Peroxide:** This ingredient often causes excessive dryness of the skin, and salicylic acid is a notorious skin irritant—both of which are found in non-natural pimple creams.

Recycle

- **Choose Companies That Care About Recycling:** Avoid companies whose products come packaged in unnecessary, excessive, or non-recyclable packaging.
- **Think About Where the Ingredients End Up:** When you purchase products with natural ingredients, not only will you be doing something good for you and your body, but you won't be sending any toxic chemicals back into the environment.

Eco-Chic Resources:
<u>Beauty</u>

Origins   http://www.origins.com
A division of cosmetic giant Estée Lauder, it is one of the best (and first) organic beauty brands.

Alima   http://alimacosmetics.com

Specializes in handcrafting mineral makeup using the purest ingredients available

drugstore.com   http://www.drugstore.com

Carries a wide selection of organic beauty products, including Jane Inc., DDF, Alba Botanica, Aura Cacia, Avalon Organics, Desert Essence, Kiss My Face

Breath Palette   http://www.breathpalette.com

Thirty-two flavors of all-natural toothpaste

beauty.com   http://beauty.com

Carries organic and natural beauty products, including John Masters Organic, Juice Beauty, Sanoflore, Trilogy, Brickhouse

Coco's Shoppe   http://cocosshoppe.com

Carries hip organic beauty (and fashion) brands like Einstein Lip Theory, Hamadi, Juara, Red Flower, The Balm

A Wild Soap Bar   http://awildsoapbar.com

Natural handmade olive oil soap

Agoo Agii   http://agooagii.com

Eco-balanced skin and body care

Dropwise   http://dropwise.com

Premium aromatherapy and organic plant-based body care

Garden of Eve Skin Care   http://garden-of-eve.com
Natural and organic skin care that is as pure as it gets!

Purely Shea   http://purelyshea.com
Purely shea organic shea butter skin care

Nature's Gate   http://naturesgate.com

JASON products   http://jason-natural.com

Trillium Organics   http://trilliumorganics.com

chapter 9

menu

Nearly half of your wedding budget will probably be spent on the reception, and a huge part of this cost is the meal you will serve your guests. Whether it's a brunch, a lunch, or a dinner, you can make a few good decisions about the ingredients that will make a positive impact. If you truly want to simplify your plans, one way to go is to have a lovely punch-and-cake reception in the mid-afternoon. This quaint but festive style of party harkens back to a less-flashy era, when our grandparents and great-grandparents were wed. Simple and elegant, there wasn't a lot of fuss—but look at how long their relationships lasted!

Hopefully you have been successful in finding a location that is open-minded and willing to work with you to incorporate unique and eco-chic ideas. Food is a big issue in our society, both the production processes and the nutritional values have come under intense scrutiny in recent years. Are carbs good or bad? What is organic, and why is it preferred? Should we be vegetarian, or is meat okay, so long as it's produced in a healthy way? I'm not a nutritionist, and I can't give you advice about what is the healthiest choice for you. I can tell you some research does show the consumption of organically grown foods to be a good way to avoid consuming toxic pesticides and fertilizers. In turn, organic food, when produced and reintroduced into the environment post-consumption, puts fewer toxic chemicals into the environment and food chain.

According to *The Environmental Magazine*, an average dinner travels 1500 miles, using energy and packaging that will ultimately go into landfills. If we buy our food from local farmers, not only will we reduce energy consumption and potential packaging waste, but your dollars will also stay within your community and strengthen the local economy. Most often, the food you buy locally is much fresher because it is usually sold within twenty-four hours of being harvested. As for the vegetarian question, I can tell you that according to the U.S. Department of Agriculture, 2500 gallons of water are spent to produce just 1 pound of meat, compared to 25 gallons to grow a pound of wheat. And this doesn't account for the vast tracts of land needed for cattle production, much of which is left barren after herds have fed there.

If you have a sweet tooth like I do, you may be distressed to know that sugar crops may be responsible for more biodiversity loss than any other crop in the world. The traditional methods for growing sugar cane result in the destruction of habitat, intensive use of water for irrigation, use of agricultural chemicals, and contaminated water. It's not just in Brazil and other far-off lands that you've never been to—it's right here in our own backyard. By all accounts, the

Florida Everglades are seriously compromised after decades of sugar cane farming. Another issue with sugar production is the often discussed lack of free trade in the industry. Opponents to the so-called "Big Sugar industry" believe that the U.S. consumer is forced to spend approximately $2.5 billion more a year than they would in other parts of the world. Basically, Americans pay two-and-a-half times the world price. (Source: *National Review Online*, Stephen Moore, April 15, 2005) One result of this price hike is the mass use of high fructose corn syrup instead of sugar. Some critics believe the proliferation of the chemically manufactured sugar replacement may be a main cause of the growing levels of obesity in the U.S.

According to the Specialty Coffee Association, Americans consume some 300 million cups of coffee every day. Globally, coffee is second only to oil in terms of dollars traded, and it has a tremendous social and ecological footprint, particularly in regions of the world that also host some of the planet's greatest, and most threatened, bio diversity. U.S. retailers such as Starbucks are creating opportunities for smaller coffee growers to sell to the larger global market, which is a good.

Chocolate may indeed be good for your health, (Source: Harvard University, 2000) but industrial production of cocoa in different tropical regions of the world results in the clearing of tropical rainforests, erosion and run-off, reduced soil fertility, contaminated crucial water supplies, and the destruction of wildlife habitat (Environmental Action website). But there are ways to avoid this destruction, and you can help make things better by starting with the food you choose to serve at your wedding. You can learn more about the food we eat and its impact on the environment at web sites like centerforfoodsafety.org.

Reduce

- **Request Organic Ingredients:** This will reduce your and the land's exposure to harmful toxic materials and provide you with more absorbable nutrients. Plus, fresh and organic foods usually taste better.
- **Consider Going Vegetarian:** Plant proteins (legumes, vegetables, grains, fruits) use fewer valuable resources—less land and water—per pound than livestock.
- **Serve Safe Salmon:** If you serve salmon, request that you serve product that has the Salmon Safe label.
- **Buy local:** Because the food didn't travel thousands of miles to reach you, local foods are better for the air, water, and soil. Your local economy and family farmers benefit too.
- **Eat seasonally:** Plan your menu around foods that are in season.
- **Choose Fish That Isn't Over-Fished:** Over-fished seafood include swordfish and bluefin tuna.
- **Have an Afternoon Affair:** Consider having a mid-afternoon punch-and-cake reception; this is a very lovely, economical, and conservation-friendly way to celebrate (and, I might add, this is how many of our grandparents did it).
- **BYOB:** Buy your own organic wine at wholesale—you'll probably pay a corkage fee, but in the end you'll save money. Most merchants will give you a discount if you buy the wine by the case.
- **Ask About Magnums:** See if you can use wine magnums—less bottles and less money for the corkage fee.
- **Make the Cake Organic:** If necessary, you can hire an outside baker (check with your venue) to bake you a delicious organic

wedding cake, and remember that square cakes go farther. You will probably still need to pay a cake-cutting fee to the location staff. Instruct your baker to make only enough cake for each guest to have one piece, so you avoid throwing any away.

- **Let Them Eat Cake:** Just serve the wedding cake as dessert—don't have a separate dessert as well (most guests won't eat both, so you'll reduce any excess waste).
- **Forget the Cake-Topper:** Avoid the wedding-themed (and cheesy) cake-toppers—they will be thrown away once the day is over. Instead, have beautiful fondant, piping, fruit, or edible flowers.
- **Serve Organic Coffee, Chocolate, and Sugar:** Ensure these items come from organic, fair-trade cocoa farmers, many of whom are found in South America along the Amazon. There are some 42,000 cocoa "cooperatives" that help small farmers get their products to market while protecting the environment and enabling them to earn a living wage. And choose to use organically grown sugar or better yet, more natural sweeteners like fruit, honey, or agave nectar.

Reuse

- **Avoid Throw-Aways:** Make sure the platters, utensils, glasses, napkins, and any other materials are not one-time-use items—for all events leading up to the wedding as well (showers, engagement parties, etc.).
- **Have a To-Go Menu:** Make small "to-go" packages of leftover items for your guests to take with them when they depart. The band might even appreciate taking a few snacks with them after

they've played their little hearts out for you and your loved ones.

Recycle

- **Don't Use Plastic:** For all of your wedding events, avoid using paper and plastic dinnerware.
- **Encourage Recycling:** When you do have items that cannot be reused, such as wine bottles, be sure they're properly recycled. Confirm this with your caterer or venue before the wedding; you won't have to worry if the place you choose has a standing policy to recycle.

Eco-Chic Resources: The Menu

Organic Food Industry Information

Eat Well Guide   http://eatwellguide.org
Resource for healthy and sustainable food

Marine Conservation Society   http://mcsuk.org

Chez Panisse   http://chezpanisse.com

Salmon Safe   http://salmonsafe.org

Organic Consumers Association   http://organicconsumers.org

Seafood Choices Alliance   http://seafoodchoices.org

EcoFish   http://www.ecofish.com

Coffee and Chocolate

Fair Coffee   http://faircoffee.com

Local Harvest   http://www.localharvest.org

Coffee Review   http://coffeereview.com

Dagoba Chocalate   http://dagobachocolate.com

Wine

Amity Vineyards   http://www.amityvineyards.com

Cooper Mountain Vineyards   http://coopermountainwine.com

Frey Vineyards   http://www.freywine.com

Diamond Organics   http://diamondorganics.com

Paradigm Winery   http://www.paradigmwinery.com

Fetzer Vineyards   http://fetzer.com

The Organic Wine Company   http://theorganicwinecompany.com

chapter 10

transportation

On your wedding day, you probably won't arrive with your groom. And if your ceremony and reception are in two different locations, you will need to find a way for the two of you to get from one place to the next. Many couples take this opportunity to arrive in style—they might rent a stretch limo or an antique Rolls Royce. Certainly the emissions of whatever vehicle you might choose will be insignificant compared to any given day on the L.A. freeway. It isn't true you can't make a difference. After all, if you combine all of the brides and grooms who get married each year, and each weekend, it's about 40,400 couples. (Condé Nast Wedding Survey 2006)

Obviously, the fossil fuel emissions add up. We all know by now the effect of automobiles—from the emissions, which impact the air we breathe, to the oil industry we rely upon to fuel our cars. Though there is positive change taking root in our society, millions of Americans still face dangerous levels of air pollution. Even with the growing pro-environmental sentiment and stronger federal and local regulations, over half of the U.S. population still live in areas that have recorded levels of smog or particle pollution that is unsafe. Exposure to particle pollution has been linked to increases in heart attacks, strokes, and emergency-room visits for asthma and cardiovascular disease. We need to continue with our aggressive changes, and let our government and industry leaders know we want more positive result.

In the grand scheme of things, your choice of transportation on your wedding day may seem like a trivial matter in the larger context

row, row, row your bride

For Alyssa Hochberg Fontaine, getting married was smooth sailing—literally. It was natural that she should choose the home of her parents in Litchfield County, Connecticut for her Summer 2005 wedding. She had, after all, spent many happy times there with her family, so it seemed the perfect choice for her to celebrate her marriage. Her choice of transportation also seemed quite natural, since her parent's house and the location, the Interlaken Inn, sat on opposite sides of a lake. Of course she would arrive and depart by boat. On the day of her wedding, Alyssa and her parents walked down to their dock to the awaiting boat. The journey across the lake was a nice quiet moment that Alyssa got to spend with her parents before the ceremony. After their celebration ended, Alyssa and her new husband, Michael Fontaine, departed by boat, with their guests waving from the shore.

of the air pollution problem. But the changes that are happening make an impact one driver at a time. According to the 2005 State of the Air Report from the American Lung Association (ALA), air pollution levels improved in many parts of the nation during the first few years of the new millennium, probably due to the changes we have been systematically making over the past decade. This reinforces the idea that what we do in our own lives can—and does—make a difference.

So yes, the choice of your vehicle on your wedding day—combined with the millions of other couples getting married—is relevant, and you can help make a difference. So instead of going for that stretch limo, or pollution-prone vintage Rolls, consider making a wiser and healthier choice. We know for certain that every individual can help improve air quality by cutting down on driving, and by choosing more eco-cars, even on your wedding day.

Reduce

- **Carpool:** Drive to and from the wedding with friends or family—you'll save money and reduce fuel emissions. It will also give you extra time to spend with the people you love. Encourage your guests to carpool, either from the hotel or from the ceremony to the reception.
- **Drive a Hybrid:** Consider using a hybrid vehicle as your getaway car—many local big-city car services are offering greener fleets.
- **Sail Away:** Speaking of fleets, arrive by boat—sailboat, rowboat, canoe, paddle boat, or even an Italian gondola!
- **Arrive on a Horse:** A horse-drawn carriage is a regal and eco-friendly way to arrive and depart in style, so long as there are horse stables nearby.

- **Ride a Bike:** Especially for a country wedding, this would be a sweet way to arrive. And did you know that they actually make bicycles out of bamboo? You could take "going green" to a whole new level.
- **Drive Your Own Car:** No hassle, and less money.
- **Drive Ethanol:** Did you know that there are almost two million ethanol-fueled cars on the market in the U.S.? These cars can use corn-based E85 ethanol fuel. If you switched to ethanol for all of your driving throughout the year, you would reduce your consumption of oil by about 16 barrels (that's about 22,800 cobs of corn). (Source: http://BP.com)
- **Take Public Transportation:** If you're in a city, what about taking public transportation? Seems strange, but imagine the great photos—not to mention stares—you'll get! Or, take a pedicab!
- **Have the Ceremony and Reception at the Same Place:** Choose to have your ceremony and reception in one location and you will cut down on emissions because no one will have to drive from one place to the other. Or even better, have your entire wedding take place at the hotel where all of your guests are staying; this works particularly well if you have chosen a resort location.

Eco-Chic Resources: Transportation

Environmental car rental   http://evrental.com

Biobling   http://biobling.com
Retrofits cars, soups them up, and makes them into biodiesel fuel cars (kind of like a "green" version of MTV's Pimp My Ride)

Enterprise Rent-A-Car   http://www.enterprise.com
They rent the Toyota Prius

EVO Limo Service   http://evolimo.com
Rent natural gas-powered limos in L.A.

Bio-Beetle   http://bio-beetle.com

Fox Rent-A-Car   http://foxrentacar.com

chapter 11

honeymoon

The average amount spent on a honeymoon is $3,700, and that's three times as much as the average U.S. adult spends on a vacation. While 37 percent of these trips are to domestic locales, a whopping 63 percent are to foreign destinations. That means you can really make a difference on a global level when you plan your honeymoon. Unfortunately 40 percent of honeymooners stay at large resorts, so much of the money they spend doesn't go into the local economies. (Source: U.S. Office of Travel and Tourism, ita.doc.gov) Often these resorts are foreign-owned and sometimes even the staff is "imported" from outside of the country. You can choose to support a locally owned resort.

Hotels are one of the largest users of energy, water, and material resources. And there are growing numbers of them making the travel industry "greener." Because so many indigenousness populations have turned to tourism as their main source of revenue, identifying the degree to which fair trade is practiced by a particular hotel or resort is also critical. The green trend has proliferated primarily at smaller independent hotels, but the large chains are paying attention, too.

Reduce

- **Take Care of the Reefs:** Did you know that, despite awareness, direct physical damage to coral reefs by divers and snorkelers continues to rise? Unfortunately, many divers neglect to consider what harm their presence within this fragile environment can cause. If you plan to go diving, first learn about the fragility of the reefs you plan to visit, and always practice "minimal impact" when around coral. There are important precautions you should also take to make sure you aren't causing harm.
- **Think Before You Go Cruising:** 10% of honeymooners go on a cruise, but did you know that one of the largest waterway polluters is the cruise ship industry? These large ships often dump raw sewage directly into the sea. It is estimated that the cruise ship industry discharges tens of thousands of pounds of sewage a day into oceans. In some waterways, in fact, cruise ship sewage represents a disproportionate percentage of the water pollution problem. Discharge into the ocean by cruise ships is not covered under the Clean Water Act, so it is often unregulated. After yielding to consumer pressure, Royal Caribbean has agreed to adopt sophisticated wastewater treatment technology to treat sewage on board, and is now installing systems throughout its entire fleet. But the jury is still out as to how widespread effective these changes will be.

- **Support Companies Doing Good:** You can go to greenho-tels.com to see if a hotel or resort supports an organization that pays fair wages and supports a community's local economy, and follows good environmental practices by using all-natural, biodegradable, and organic soaps, lotions, and cleaning products.
- **Go On a Volunteer Vacation:** Consider making a real impact and go on a volunteer vacation. You might go to an off-the-beaten path location and assist with a variety of different tasks. You could do anything from teaching kids to swim, to building a house, to studying wildlife. Trips usually last anywhere from two to four weeks, and locations include Costa Rica, Ghana, Tanzania, Guatemala, and Russia. For more information, go to volunteervacation.org.

Reuse

- **Water Conservation:** Make sure guests are given the option to re-use towels and keep their sheets for more than one night to reduce water consumption. Find out if the showers, toilets, and sinks are low-pressure and low-flush (this is particularly critical in water-deprived areas such as the Southwestern U.S. or sub-Saharan Africa).

Recycle

- **Find Out What the Recycling Program Is:** Go to a hotel with an ambitious recycling program.

an italian romance

Sarah Walsh Esposito and Phil Esposito were married in Fiesole, Italy in July 2004. For their honeymoon, they decided to continue their Italian adventure by staying in a rented apartment on the Amalfi Coast. Close to the fabulous island of Capri, they devoured the culture, food, music, and flavor of this most beautiful part of Europe. They shopped for food at the local market, feasting on fresh mozzarella and prosciutto just like the locals do. In the evenings, they would venture out to the many locally owned restaurants for a true taste of the region. It was relaxing and magnificent, and they relished their exposure to what life in Italy really is. And they also got the satisfaction of knowing that their dollars were going to the local businesses that are so integral to sustaining the economy of this glorious part of Europe.

Ten Amazing Eco-Chic Honeymoons

1. Visit Big Sky Country

The Papoose Creek Lodge in Cameron, Montana, is a gourmet experience in the great outdoors. With a main lodge and comfortable private cabins, you can spend your time exploring the beautiful terrain and dining on world-class cuisine. Everything is done with an eco-focus—from naturalist talks, to horseback riding, to the local ingredients used in all of the meals. CONTACT: papoosecreek.com, 1-888-674-3030

2. Belize

Take an eco-approach to exploring coral reefs in Belize. You can be a part of the efforts to collect data about the coral reef environment along a piece of the largest barrier reef in the Western Hemisphere. Stay in beach cabanas with private bathrooms at Blackbird Caye, Belize. CONTACT: Oceanic Society, oceanic-society.org, 1-800-326-7491

3. Africa

High-end tourism lodges that enable the local communities to work their way out of extreme poverty are cropping up in Africa. The Guludo Beach Lodge in Mozambique was the first of these lodges to open. Guludo Beach Lodge overlooks one of the best beaches in Mozambique. You can dive in the pristine coral reefs, explore the islands, and soak up the rich local culture while taking in the vast African landscape. CONTACT: bespokeExperience.com, 011-01323-766655

4. Fiji

The Fiji Resort is owned by the son of the late Jacques Cousteau. Jean-Michel is dedicated to sharing his love of land, ocean, and culture, and his commitment to preservation. Jean-Michel's passion for the indigenous people of Fiji, their culture, traditions, warmth, and natural hospitality have led him to create an eco-friendly resort with a unique environmental philosophy. CONTACT: Fijiresort.com, 1-800-246-3454

5. San Francisco

The Hotel Triton in San Francisco has twenty-four rooms with organic cotton towels and energy-saving motion-sensor lights. CONTACT: hoteltriton.com, 1-415-394-0500

6. Maldives

Coco Palm Dhuni Kolhu is located on Dhuni Kolhu Island in the Baa Atoll of the Maldives. Surrounded by white sandy beaches, the hotel comprises 98 luxury villas, including twelve lagoon villas with open-air garden bathrooms, private terraces, and large plunge pools. CONTACT: cocopalm.com/dhunikolhu/location.htm, 960-23-00-11

7. Bora Bora

Located on a private white sand in Bora Bora's turquoise lagoon, the Eden Beach Hotel opened in 2001 with just fifteen bungalows. This environmentally friendly hotel relies on solar energy and practices recycling and autonomous water management. An ideal place to get away from it all. CONTACT: borabora.net, 689 605760

8. Argentina

Yacutinga Lodge is an environmentally friendly property featuring a private wildlife nature reserve located in the heart of the Argentinean rainforest, surrounded by the Iguazú National Park. The wildlife and nature reserve area, covering 1400 acres, is part of the protected rainforest shared by Brazil and Argentina and known as the "green corridor." The lodge has comfortable and uniquely designed suites, a restaurant, bars, and a pool—all of which are designed to be in perfect balance with the surrounding nature. CONTACT: www.yacutinga.com

9. St. John, Virgin Islands

The Maho Bay Camps have 114 ocean-side tent-cottages are the ultimate in environmental retreats. The island of St. John is itself a veritable nature preserve, and this resort is considered to be the best eco-resort in the Caribbean. Enjoy beautiful beaches, hiking trails, and exceptional views of the ocean and Virgin Islands National Park. CONTACT: Maho.org, 1-800-392-9004

10. Six Senses Spa and Resorts

With multiple resorts, mainly concentrated in Southeast Asia and parts of Europe, this resort company has the business ethics that all tourism professionals should strive for. Their mission is to build and operate resorts that are physically in harmony with their natural surroundings, as well as sustainable practices. There are a number of beautiful resorts to choose from. CONTACT: sixsenses.com

Eco-Chic Resources: <u>The Honeymoon</u>

Responsible Tourism Information

The Blue Flag Programme   http://blueflag.org

The Blue Flag is an exclusive eco-label awarded to over 3100 beaches and marinas in 36 countries across Europe, South Africa, Morocco, New Zealand, Canada, and the Caribbean in 2006. The Blue Flag promotes sustainable development at beaches and marinas.

Green Globe   http://greenglobe.org

Green Globe has environmental information about international destinations and business outlining responsible behavior across economic, social, and environmental management.   The site will help you plan your honeymoon— the Green Globe label is used by participating resorts, tours, and rental car companies.

Oceana   http://stopcruisepollution.com

The International Ecotourism Society

http://www.ecotourism.org

United Nations Environment Programme   http://unep.org

Project AWARE   http://projectaware.org

Reef Relief   http://reefrelief.org

Conservation International   http://www.conservation.org

Audobon Green Leaf Eco-Rating Program

http://www.audoboninternational.org

Travel Companies

Travelroots   http://travelroots.com
  Holidays that do good for the world

Blue Ventures   http://www.blueventures.org
  Marine Conservation Holidays

Tourism Partnership   http://tourismpartnership.org

Sustainable Travel International   http://sustainabletravel.com

Bespoke Experience   http://bespokeexperience.com

Eco-Resorts and Hotels

El Monte Sagrado Resort   http://elmontesagrado.com
Taos, New Mexico

Campi ya Kanzi   http://www.maasai.com

A fabulous ranch in Kenya developed by the local Maasi. The entire property is environmentally friendly, built from local materials without cutting down any trees.

Cree Village Ecolodge   http://www.creevillage.com

Moose Factory Island, Ontario

Forest House Eco-Lodge   http://www.foresthouse.ca

Air Ronge, Saskatchewan

Arbor House   http://arbor-house.com

National award-winning inn and model for sustainable tourism in Madison, Wisconsin

chapter 12

married life

Of course, being eco-chic doesn't end with the wedding and the honeymoon. If you're like most newlyweds, you will be combining your households, purchasing new furniture, and even purchasing your first home together. According to TheKnot.com, more than 32 percent of newlyweds plan to buy a home sometime during the first five years of marriage. Thus, brides and grooms represent one of the largest markets for home purchases in the U.S.

The building industry is at the forefront of sustainable practices—due in large part to its dependence on natural resources. Finding green buildings in any given city in the world is pretty common at this point. A green building, according to builditgreen.org, a non-profit industry resource, is "sited, designed, constructed, and operated to enhance the well-being of occupants, and to minimize negative impacts on the community and natural environment." According to EPA reports, the air in new homes can be up to ten times more polluted than outside air due to volatile organic compounds (VOCs) and other chemicals used in product manufacturing. Homes that follow green-building guidelines use healthier paints and building materials, and adhere to stricter gas emission and ventilation requirements, improving the quality of a home's indoor environment.

Green building can also mean that fewer non-renewable natural resources are used for construction. According to the U.S. Department of Energy's Center for Sustainable Development, buildings consume 40 percent of the world's total energy, 25 percent of its wood harvest, and 16 percent of its water. Compared to traditional construction, a green-built home takes some of this pressure off the environment.

Other benefits to building green:
• Provides a healthier and more comfortable environment
• Improves long-term economic performance
• Incorporates energy- and water-efficient technologies
• Uses recycled materials
• Reduces construction and demolition waste
• Brings higher resale value
• Better water and energy efficiency
• Improves indoor air quality
• Easier to maintain and built to last
• Reduces environmental impact

You will probably need some furniture to go in that new house. But, before you buy that king-size bed, make sure you know about the pieces you will be bringing into your life. Many of these items will be around for a very long time. You may not be aware of the fact that many toxic materials are used in the traditional furniture-making process, and many of these are known to decrease indoor air quality. In fact, the U.S. Environmental Protection Agency is seriously considering regulating furniture production with a program called the Environmental Technology Verification Project.

Many homeowners don't realize how much energy they waste because they have windows that aren't installed properly or that aren't made of the right kind of material. One estimate by the U.S. Department of Energy states that 25 percent of the energy used to heat and cool buildings goes right out the window—literally.

One thing is for certain—there are important steps you should take before you move into your new home, or even before you purchase your new home. We spend about 80 percent of our time indoors and oftentimes the quality of our indoor environment is more polluted than the outdoor environment, because it is an enclosed space. But you can certainly educate yourself and make better choices that will result in a healthier home for you and your growing family.

Reduce

- **Use Timers:** Put your air conditioning/heaters on timers. Lights that go on and off automatically will turn the lights off when you aren't in the room.
- **Avoid Toxic Paints:** Regular paint harbors volatile organic compounds (VOCs), like benzene and acetone, which have been linked to respiratory ailments and the destruction of the ozone layer. Look for low- or zero-VOC paints from Benjamin Moore or Sherwin Williams.

- **Conserve Water:** Use low-flush toilets/low-water pressure faucets to conserve water.
- **Conserve Energy:** Use compact fluorescent lightbulbs and halogen lamps because they save energy. They last ten times longer and use 25 percent less energy than regular. Make sure your windows provide proper insulation; casement windows are the most efficient for energy savings. When you purchase any electrical items, look for the Energy Star label. This program is designed to help consumers determine the energy efficiency of home electrics.
- **Buy Green Furniture:** Avoid furniture made from pressure-treated wood. Find furniture made with toxic-free alternatives, such as California-based Tamalpais NatureWorks. They use toxic-free finishes, paints, stains, and waxes from BioShield, which makes its products out of citrus peel extracts, essential oils, tree resins, bee waxes, and natural pigments. Invest in organic furniture and fabrics—Massachusetts-based Furnature uses organic upholstery. You can even find eco-friendly beds from Green Culture, not to mention nightstands, tables, dressers, and armoires. Verify that the furniture you buy is eco-friendly with the SmartWood forest certification program. Forest Stewardship Council (FSC) also certifies furniture that was made from sustainably harvested, well-managed forests.
- **Use Green Building Materials:** This includes wood that has been certified by the Forest Stewardship Council because it comes from forests managed according to social and environmental criteria. You can also choose from a variety of alternative materials, like cork or tile flooring (rather than vinyl), or wool and (organic) cotton carpet (rather than synthetic, which cannot be recycled and is non-biodegradable). Ask a green building specialist to help you determine how sustainable and healthy

your new home is. He or she might also be able to give you a plan to make your home more green. You can find more information at the Energy and Environmental Building Association (eeba.org).

- **Reduce Air Pollution:** You might be surprised to learn that the pollution generated from cutting grass for an hour with a gasoline-powered lawn mower is equivalent to a 100-mile automobile ride. More than 54 million Americans mow their lawns every week in the warmer months, and this alone may be as much as 5 percent of the nation's air pollution, according to the EPA. Buy an electronic mower, or maybe even a solar-powered "auto mower" from Husqvarna ($2,000), or the solar-powered mulching mower from Gaiam ($795). You might also consider a natural, indigenous landscaping rather than hard to maintain manicured lawns. Xeriscape is an example of this in the semi-arid West and Southwestern U.S. Xeriscaping is a way to create landscaping that doesn't require supplemental irrigation. For more information, go to xeriscape.org.

Reuse

- **Get Crafty:** Shop flea markets, or even drive around to see what kind of stuff people put out on the curb every day. Use some creative inspiration and a little elbow grease to transform throw-away furniture into one-of-a-kind pieces you will enjoy for years to come.
- **Take Care of Your Things:** Mom was right—you really should take good care of everything you have to keep it from filling up a landfill. Keep appliances clean, including the oven, stove,

toaster, and refrigerator, and you'll avoid having time-worn items that you just have to get rid of.

Recycle

• **Get Educated:** Find out what the recycling program is in your town, when pick-up is, and how items must be sorted. Create a recycling area in your house and make sure everything that can be recycled is. Also, don't buy packaged items unless they have the recyclable label—there are so many options now that can be recycled that you should support those brands making a positive change.

Eco-Chic Resources: Married Life

Food and Beverage

Lakewinds Natural Foods   http://www.lakewinds.com
An online coop where you can purchase natural, farm-grown, and organic food

Kunde Estate   http://kunde.com
Grows and sells sustainably grown wine

Etica Fair Trade   http://eticafairtrade.com
Fair-trade wine and gifts

Food for Thought   http://giftsthatmatter.com
Gifts that matter

Himalasalt   http://himalasalt.com
Ethically sourced Himalayan sea salt and natural foods

Future Green   http://futuregreen.net
Future Green features organic products that support organic
farming and agriculture.

Sustainable Table   http://sustainabletable.org

Food Routes   http://foodroutes.org

100 Mile Diet   http://100milediet.org

Water

BIOTA   http://biotaspringwater.com
Spring water is the world's first bottled water/beverage packaged in a Planet Friendly™ bottle.

Belu Water   http://www.belu.org
British bottled water with compostable plastic bottle made
from corn; all profits go to clean-water programs.

Energy

Verde Energy   http://verdeenergy.com
Renewable energy contractor services

Real Goods   http://realgoods.com
Sustainable energy products for the home

Bag-E-Wash   http://bag-e-wash.com
Wash and dry zipper-style bags in your dishwasher

Best Filters   http://bestfilters.com
Top-rated air filters, water purifiers

Energy Star   http://energystar.gov

Positive Energy   http://positiveenergy.com

Cleaning

Green Clean, Inc.   http://greenclean.biz
Increasing awareness about chemical-free cleaning products

Husqvarna Group   http://husqvarna.com

Seventh Generation   http://www.seventhgeneration.com

Earth Friendly Products   http://ecos.com

GreenEarth Cleaning   http://greenearthcleaning.com

EcoLogic Solutions   http://ecologicsolutions.com

Sustainable Spaces   http://sustainablespaces.com

Home Design and Décor

Daiseye   http://daiseye.com
An eclectic marketplace offering earth-friendly products
to enhance your living space

A Natural Home   http://anaturalhome.com
Affordable organic bedding and furniture

Green Alcove   http://thegreenalcove.com
Eco-friendly home accessories and gifts

Green Logic   http://green-logic.net
Sustainable products for the home, solutions for daily life

Paloma Pottery   http://palomapottery.com
Recycled glass-infused pottery

Spirit Hills   http://www.spirithills.com
Twenty-five easy home improvements that save you green

Tilonia   http://tilonia.com
Tilonia home textiles bring the color and spice of India

Viva Terra   http://www.vivaterra.com

Bamboo Handicraft   http://www.bamboohandicraft.com

Tivoli Home   http://tivolihome.com

Scandanavian Designs   http://scandinaviandesigns.com

Kvadrat   http://www.kvadrat.dk
Danish fabric designers dedicated to minimizing their environmental impact

Poppy Cotton   http://poppycotton.com
Furnishings using recycled fabrics

Feather Your Nest   http://shopfeatheryournest.com

Adelphia Paper Hangings http://www.adelphiapaperhangings.com
Acid-free, traditionally made wallpaper

Casa Natura   http://casanaturainc.com
Healthy bedding and other products for the home

Ten Thousand Villages   http://www.tenthousandvillages.com
Handcrafted, fair-trade items for the home

Furniture

Maria Yee   http://mariayee.com
Designed and manufactured according to environmental principles. They also have a patent-pending special renewable bamboo product for sustainable furniture, BambooTimbre(tm).

Furnature   http://furnature.com

Plyboo   http://plyboo.com

American Bamboo Society   http://americanbamboo.org

Environmental Bamboo   http://bamboocentral.org
Foundation

Bamboo Style   http://bamboostyle.net

Clothing and Accessories

AFESIP Fair Fashion   http://afesip.org

Asian-inspired clothing; lovely creative alternatives for brides-maid, or even wedding gowns. This organization combats trafficking of women and children for sex slavery in southeast Asia.

Bamboosa   http://www.bamboosa.com

Soft and protective bamboo clothing

Hiroko Kurihara   http://hirokokurihara.com

A home textiles designer whose beautiful products are well-crafted, unique designs. The company philosophy is to build responsibility and conscientiousness in consumption and to foster a model of responsible corporate citizenship.

Studio 1am   http://studio1am.com

They explore new ideas in materials and processes through projects like recycled jewelry and adaptable objects.

Linda Loudermilk   http://www.lindaloudermilk.com

Luxury eco(tm) redefines sustainability with design that gives back to the earth.

Del Forte Denim   http://delforte.com

Del Forte Denim is designed for the eco-chic woman who is transforming the face of fashion. Made in the USA with 100 percent organic cotton.

Intoxica Jeans   http://intoxica-jeans.com
Made of materials that are both long lasting and environmentally sound

Blue Canoe   http://www.bluecanoe.com
Fashionable organic clothing options

Fashion-Incubator   http://www.fashion-incubator.com

It's Our Nature   http://itsournature.com

Finance and Career

Krull & Company   http://krullandcompany.com
Socially responsible investments

Green Key Real Estate   http://greenkeyhomes.com

Organic Coupons   http://organiccoupons.org

Gardening and Pest Control

All Natural Lawns   http://allnaturallawns.com
Organic lawn care

Hot Pepper Wax   http://hotpepperwax.com
Natural insect and animal repellant

Naturalyards   http://naturalyards.com
Progressive Gardens

American Lawn Mower   http://reelin.com

Acknowledgments

Thanks to my wonderful husband David, who is the best thing that ever happened to me. My parents, Margaret and Vance, for supporting me and my (sometimes hair brained) ideas for practically forever. Jamie, Heather, Meaghan, Rachael, you all mean so very much to me. Grandma Lucille, you've always inspired me with your creativity and style—and someday I'll learn to do upholstery too! Grandma Marion, thanks for sharing your love and appreciation of the natural world, the birds, flowers, and plants with me all through my life. Jane and David, you guys are so wonderful and fun and supportive. Cecile, thanks for being such a great mother-in-law. Thanks to Andrea Au and Alyssa Smith for guiding me through this process so kindly. My wonderful friends, especially Anne and Tara, you both supported me from the very beginning and encouraged me all along the way. Thanks to everyone at FB and H.P., and a special thank you to Meaghan Anderson for helping me with the research and editing.

appendix

eco-chic resources

Beauty · 129

Candles · 130

Charitable Alternatives to Gifts · 130

Cleaning · 131

Clothing and Accessories · 131

Coffee, Tea, and Treats · 133

Donations · 134

Eco-Resorts and Hotels · 134

Energy · 135

Fabric and Trim · 136

Fashion Accessories · 136

Fashion Apparel · 137

Finance and Career · 139

Flowers · 139

Food and Beverages 140

Furniture 141

Gardening and Pest Control 141

Getting Started 142

Gift Certificate Programs 143

Home Design and Décor 144

Jewelry 146

Locations 149

Online Registries 150

Organic Food Industry Information 151

Paper Industry 151

Paper Stationers 152

Printer Cartridge Recycling 152

Ribbon 153

Tourism Information 153

Transportation 154

Travel Companies 155

Vintage, Craft, Reusable, 155
and Fair-Trade Items

Water 156

Wedding Invitations 157

Wine 157

Beauty

Origins   http://www.origins.com

A division of cosmetic giant Estée Lauder, it is one of the best (and first) organic beauty brands.

Alima   http://alimacosmetics.com

Specializes in handcrafting mineral makeup using the purest ingredients available

drugstore.com   http://www.drugstore.com

Carries a wide selection of organic beauty products, including Jane Inc., DDF, Alba Botanica, Aura Cacia, Avalon Organics, Desert Essence, Kiss My Face

Breath Palette   http://www.breathpalette.com

Thirty-two flavors of all natural toothpaste

beauty.com   http://beauty.com

Carries organic and natural beauty products, including John Masters Organic, Juice Beauty, Sanoflore, Trilogy, Brickhouse

Coco's Shoppe   http://cocosshoppe.com

Carries hip organic beauty (and fashion) brands like Einstein Lip Theory, Hamadi, Juara, Red Flower, The Balm

A Wild Soap Bar   http://awildsoapbar.com

Natural handmade olive oil soap

Agoo Agii   http://agooagii.com
Eco-balanced skin and body care

Dropwise   http://dropwise.com
Premium aromatherapy and organic plant-based body care

Garden of Eve Skin Care   http://garden-of-eve.com
Natural and organic skin care that is as pure as it gets!

Purely Shea   http://purelyshea.com
Purely shea organic shea butter skin care

Nature's Gate   http://naturesgate.com

JASON products   http://jason-natural.com

Trillium Organics   http://trilliumorganics.com

Candles

Cox and Cox   http://coxandcox.co.uk
Bird candles, clip-on butterflies, linen ribbon, and more

Greenspace Candles   http://greenspacecandles.com

Charitable Alternatives to Gifts

Be the Change   http://bethechange.org

I Do Foundation   http://www.idofoundation.org

Just Give   http://www.justgive.org

Cleaning

Green Clean, Inc.   http://greenclean.biz
Increasing awareness about chemical-free cleaning products

Husqvarna Group   http://husqvarna.com

Seventh Generation   http://www.seventhgeneration.com

Earth Friendly Products   http://ecos.com

GreenEarth Cleaning   http://greenearthcleaning.com

EcoLogic Solutions   http://ecologicsolutions.com

Sustainable Spaces   http://sustainablespaces.com

Clothing and Accessories

AFESIP Fair Fashion   http://afesip.org
Asian-inspired clothing; lovely creative alternatives for bridesmaid, or even wedding gowns. This organization combats trafficking of women and children for sex slavery in southeast Asia.

Bamboosa   http://www.bamboosa.com
Soft and protective bamboo clothing

Hiroko Kurihara   http://hirokokurihara.com

A home textiles designer whose beautiful products are well-crafted, unique designs. The company philosophy is to build responsibility and conscientiousness in consumption and to foster a model of responsible corporate citizenship.

Studio 1am   http://studio1am.com

They explore new ideas in materials and processes through projects like recycled jewelry and adaptable objects.

Linda Loudermilk   http://www.lindaloudermilk.com

Luxury eco(tm) redefines sustainability with design that gives back to the earth.

Del Forte Denim   http://delforte.com

Del Forte Denim is designed for the eco-chic woman who is transforming the face of fashion. Made in the USA with 100 percent organic cotton.

Intoxica Jeans   http://intoxica-jeans.com

Made of materials that are both long lasting and environmentally sound

Blue Canoe   http://www.bluecanoe.com

Fashionable organic clothing options

Fashion-Incubator   http://www.fashion-incubator.com

It's Our Nature   http://itsournature.com

Coffee, Tea and Treats

Inspired Brew   http://inspiredbrew.com

Sells tea through their "Charitea" program, which supports efforts to eliminate child labor in Bolivian mines. Give packets of tea for wedding favors.

June Taylor Organic Preserves   http://junetaylorjams.com

Purveyors of fine artisanal food, and they work with local family-owned farms

Good Harvest Market   http://goodharvestmarket.com

You can give the gift of health with an organic fruit basket for your wedding guests or for out-of-town guests in their hotel rooms. They can arrange gift baskets and boxes with any theme and price.

Green Mountain Coffee   http://greenmountaincoffee.com

The Republic of Tea   http://republicoftea.com

Dagoba Organic Chocolate   http://dagobachocolate.com

Rococo Chocolates   http://rococochocolates.com

Fair Coffee   http://faircoffee.com

Local Harvest   http://www.localharvest.org

Coffee Review   http://coffeereview.com

Donations

American Diabetes Association   http://diabetes.org

Make a donation instead of giving out favors and you'll get a card from the foundations that you can give to your guests to let them know about the donation.

UNICEF   http://unicef.org

When you make a donation, they will provide you with tent cards that you can feature at your wedding.

CO2Balance   http://co2balance.com

Give your guests a real planted tree—actually, a certificate that says a tree was planted on their behalf.

The CarbonNeutral Company   http://www.carbonneutral.com

Eco-Resorts and Hotels

El Monte Sagrado Resort   http://elmontesagrado.com
Taos, New Mexico

Campi ya Kanzi   http://www.maasai.com

A fabulous ranch in Kenya developed by the local Maasi. The entire property is environmentally friendly, built from local materials without cutting down any trees.

Cree Village Ecolodge   http://creevillage.com
Moose Factory Island, Ontario

Forest House Eco-Lodge   http://www.foresthouse.ca
Air Ronge, Saskatchewan

Arbor House   http://arbor-house.com
National award-winning inn and model for sustainable tourism in Madison, Wisconsin

Energy

Verde Energy   http://verdeenergy.com
Renewable energy contractor services

Real Goods   http://realgoods.com
Sustainable energy products for the home

Bag-E-Wash   http://bag-e-wash.com
Wash and dry zipper-style bags in your dishwasher

Best Filters   http://bestfilters.com
Top-rated air filters, water purifiers

Energy Star   http://energystar.gov

Positive Energy   http://positiveenergy.com

Fabric and Trim

Sustainable Cotton   http://sustainablecotton.org

Has resources and information about why you should buy organic cotton, and where you can get organic cotton products

Aurora Silk   http://aurorasilk.com

Sells silk fabric, organic cotton fabric, hemp fabric, and rayon in case you choose to have a designer make your dress for you. You can request fabric samples before you place a larger order.

Repro Depot   http://reprodepot.com

Appliqué and fabric to spiff up a dress and make it wedding-worthy

Hemp Traders   http://hemptraders.com

Ingeo Fibers   http://ingeofibers.com

Jasco Fabrics   http://jascofabrics.com

NUI Organics   http://nuiorganics.com

The Hemp Store   http://www.thehempstore.co.uk

Fashion Accessories

Colette Malouf   http://colettemalouf.com

Beautiful ideas and designs if you want to be a little different

Bon Bon Oiseau   http://bonbonoiseau.com

Bonbon's famous handcrafted feather, leather, and chain corsages and tiny hair adornments can transform your bridal apparel into dazzling pieces.

B Jewelry   http://bjewelry.net

Hair clips with flower adornments, bridesmaid jewelry

Madame Fancy Pants   http://madamefancypants.com

Beautiful jewelry made from found items

Rose Flash   http://roseflash.ca

Fashion Apparel

Swati Argade   http://swatiargade.com

Her dresses are so beautiful they could easily be worn by bridesmaids, or even as a unique bridal gown.

The Dressmarket   http://www.thedressmarket.net

Used and some samples are available; they have a pretty good selection

Emer Maher Dowling   http://emermaherdowling.com

Lovely eco-chic items that are definitely not your typical wedding fare

Boll Organic   http://bollorganic.com

Organic cotton men's shirts

The Glass Slipper Project   http://glassslipperproject.org

If you donate your dress to them, it will go to a high school senior who can't afford to buy a dress for her prom.

Annatarian   http://annatarian.com

Hip California design company that makes eco-bridal wear

The Bridal Garden   http://bridalgarden.org

Sells designer dresses at a deep discount to benefit Sheltering Arms Children's Services

Making Memories Breast Cancer Foundation
                              http://makingmemories.org

Gently worn designer dresses; sales benefit breast cancer foundation (brides against breast cancer)

Conscious Clothing   http://getconscious.com

Stylish hemp/silk wedding gowns and bridesmaid dresses; each dress is cut and sewn to order, with attention to detail

AFESIP Fair Fashion   http://afesip.org

Asian-inspired clothing; lovely creative alternatives for bridesmaid dresses, or even wedding gowns. This organization combats trafficking of women and children for sex slavery in southeast Asia.

Loomstate   http://loomstate.org

Finance and Career

Krull & Company   http://krullandcompany.com
  Socially responsible investments

Green Key Real Estate   http://greenkeyhomes.com

Organic Coupons   http://organiccoupons.org

Flowers

Organic Bouquet   http://www.organicbouquet.com
  California Organic Flowers. Organic flowers and gifts. Shipped
  next day

Blume Box   http://blumebox.com
  They sell pretty colored boxes that are a great cost-effective
  way to add color and style to the flowers—boxes can be reused
  or recycled.

Jude Miller   http://judemiller.com
  Resource for handcrafted paper flowers

PANNA (Pesticide Action Network
North America)   http://panna.org

Homeless Gardenc Project   http://homelessgardenproject.org

Manic Organics Flowers http://www.manicorganicsflowers.com

Seabreeze Organic Farm   http://www.seabreezed.com

Local Harvest   http://www.localharvest.org

Food and Beverages

Lakewinds Natural Foods   http://www.lakewinds.com
An online coop where you can purchase natural, farm-grown, and organic food

Kunde Estate   http://kunde.com
Grows and sells sustainably grown wine

Etica Fair Trade   http://eticafairtrade.com
Fair-trade wine and gifts

Food for Thought   http://giftsthatmatter.com
Gifts that matter

Himalasalt   http://himalasalt.com
Ethically sourced Himalayan sea salt and natural foods

Future Green   http://futuregreen.net
Future Green features organic products that support organic farming and agriculture.

Sustainable Table   http://sustainabletable.org

Food Routes   http://foodroutes.org

100 Mile Diet   http://100milediet.org

Furniture

Maria Yee   http://mariayee.com
Designed and manufactured according to environmental principles. They also have a patent-pending special renewable bamboo product for sustainable furniture, BambooTimbre(tm).

Furnature   http://furnature.com

Plyboo   http://plyboo.com

American Bamboo Society   http://americanbamboo.org

Environmental Bamboo   http://bamboocentral.org
Foundation

Bamboo Style   http://bamboostyle.net

Gardening and Pest Control

All Natural Lawns   http://allnaturallawns.com
Organic lawn care

Hot Pepper Wax   http://hotpepperwax.com
Natural insect and animal repellant

Naturalyards   http://naturalyards.com
Progressive Gardens

American Lawn Mower   http://reelin.com

Getting Started

Organic Weddings   http://organicweddings.com
Michelle Kozin was ahead of the curve when she published her book a number of years ago.

Green Weddings, California   http://greenweddings.net
An online resource, based in California, with links to a variety of green wedding resources

Conscious Consumer Marketplace http://www.newdream.org
The Center for a New American Dream's Conscious Consumer Marketplace makes it easier for you to buy environmentally and socially responsible items for your wedding—and for your life.

Zerofootprint   http://zerofootprint.net
Information, products, and services for green consumers

More Hip Than Hippie   http://morehipthanhippie.com
Resources for a cool green lifestyle

Great Green Weddings   http://greatgreenwedding.com

An eco-minded wedding site with information about everything from wedding favors to honeymoons.

Choose to Reuse

Written by Nikki Goldbeck and David Goldbeck

An Encyclopedia of Services, Businesses, Tools & Charitable Programs That Facilitate Reuse

Cradle to Cradle

Written by William McDonough and Michael Braungart

This book offers compelling examples of corporations that are not just doing less harm—they're actually doing some good for the environment and their neighborhoods, and making more money in the process.

Gift Certificate Programs

Poppy Cotton   http://poppycotton.com

Poppy Cotton's vibrant pop art-era floral pieces for the home are handmade using vintage fabrics, including everything from napkins and silk kerchiefs to curtains and tablecloths. You can't register online, but you can request gift certificates from the store.

Green Glass   http://greenglass.org
Company that converts empty, discarded bottles into beautiful glassware. They do not have a registry, but you can request gift certificates from your friends and family.

3R Living   http://3rliving.com
A home decor and lifestyle store dedicated to the principles of reducing waste, reusing unwanted or discarded materials, and recycling. They do not have a registry, but you can request gift certificates in lieu of gifts.

Drop Soul   http://dropsoul.com
A store filled with sustainable and cruelty-free products. Your guests can purchase gift certificates for you.

Home Design and Décor

Daiseye   http://daiseye.com
An eclectic marketplace offering earth-friendly products to enhance your living space

A Natural Home   http://anaturalhome.com
Affordable organic bedding and furniture

Green Alcove   http://thegreenalcove.com
Eco-friendly home accessories and gifts

Green Logic   http://green-logic.net
Sustainable products for the home, solutions for daily life

Paloma Pottery   http://palomapottery.com
Recycled glass-infused pottery

Spirit Hills   http://www.spirithills.com
Twenty-five easy home improvements that save you green

Tilonia   http://tilonia.com
Tilonia home textiles bring the color and spice of India

Viva Terra   http://www.vivaterra.com

Bamboo Handicraft   http://www.bamboohandicraft.com

Tivoli Home   http://tivolihome.com

Scandanavian Designs   http://scandinaviandesigns.com

Kvadrat   http://www.kvadrat.dk
Danish fabric designers dedicated to minimizing their
environmental impact

Poppy Cotton   http://poppycotton.com
Furnishings using recycled fabrics

Feather Your Nest   http://shopfeatheryournest.com

Adelphia Paper Hangings http://www.adelphiapaperhangings.com
Acid-free, traditionally made wallpaper

Casa Natura   http://casanaturainc.com
Healthy bedding and other products for the home

Ten Thousand Villages   http://www.tenthousandvillages.com
Handcrafted, fair-trade items for the home

Jewelry

Council for Responsible Jewellery Practices
http://responsiblejewellery.com
Founded in May 2005 by members of the jewellery industry, the organization is committed to promoting responsible business practices throughout the industry from mine to retail.

Laurel Denise   http://laureldenise.com
Handmade, custom-made jewelry pieces
There are wide-ranging social and environmental problems linked to the global jewelery supply chain—from child labor and the exploitation of indigenous people to environmental degradation and disaster.

Cred Jewellery   http://cred.tv
Committed to providing a positive fair trade alternative for jewellery that pays special attention to human rights, labor standards, and care for the environment

Brilliant Earth   http://brilliantearth.com
Sells conflict-free diamonds

Green Karat   http://greenkarat.com

Uses recycled gold for all of its jewelry. They get their precious metals from objects like used jewelry and electronics.

Leber Jewelry   http://leberjeweler.com

Sells only non-conflict, free trade, and non-dirty gold items

Lee Bell Designs   http://www.fromthesky.com

For wide selection of classic, vintage style rings with Moissanite

Sumiche Jewelry Co.   http://sumiche.com

Hand-crafted custom jewelry made from sustainable mined gold and platinum

Corporacion Oro Verde or Green Gold

http://greengold-oroverde.org

Sells eco-friendly wedding jewelry and considers itself to be an investment in the conservation of bio-diversity

The Signet Group   http://kay.com

http://www.sterlingjewelers.com

Parent company of Sterling and Kay Jewelers; pledges to sell only non-dirty gold

Vancleef and Arpels   http://www.vancleef-arpels.com

Founding member of The Council for Responsible Jewelry Practices. Other members:

Fortunoff   http://fortunoff.com

Cartier   http://cartier.com

Piaget   http://www.piaget.com

Zales   http://zales.com

Tiffany & Co.   http://www.tiffany.com
Supports the Green Gold Program through the environmental
program of its foundation. They've pledged to sell only Green
Gold, as well as certified non-conflict diamonds.

Seraglia Couture Gems and Jewelery   http://seraglia.com
Seraglia couture uses antique, old, reclaimed, and unexpected
materials to create lasting heirloom pieces. They will work to
commission individual pieces, and will include your own items,
stones, or metals if desired.

Stephen Einhorn   http://www.stepheneinhorn.co.uk
An ethically responsible company that only uses manufacturers
and materials that are eco-friendly and socially responsible

Verde Rocks!   http://gwen-davis.com
A completely sustainable jewelry line using only the most natural and organic materials such as rare Timber Bamboo, rare
unused vintage beads, and antique Swarovski crystals

Coco's Shoppe   http://cocosshoppe.com

Diamond Nexus   http://www.DiamondNexusLabs.com

White Sapphire   http://www.TheNaturalSapphireCompany.com

| Cubic Zirconia | http://www.czfantasy.com |
| Russian Diamonds | http://www.russianbrilliants.net |

Locations

Green Hotels Association   http://greenhotels.com
  Lists participating eco-designated locations, both national
  and international destinations, to help you select a place that
  focuses on sustainability. Use this as a cross-reference to find
  out how green your venue is.

The Knot   http://theknot.com
  Has a really good local venue search function, but you'll have
  to check on how eco-friendly specific locations are

The Wedding Channel   http://weddingchannel.com
  Search for venues, small and large, state by state

Unique Venues   http://www.uniquevenues.com
  Has a research function that let's you search for locations in
  the U.S. and abroad. You can even check for places based on
  capacity and proximity to an airport.

Gathering Guide   http://gatheringguide.com
  Find an event location, for the ceremony and the reception,
  anywhere in the country.

Online Registries

GreenSage   http://greensage.com
A wedding registry with gifts that are energy efficient, non-toxic, recycled, reclaimed, naturally resourced, and biodegradable

Global Exchange   http://gxonlionestore.org
Register for all things ethical

Satara   http://www.satara-inc.com
Specializes in organic and natural-fiber products for the home. They have an online gift registry, which you can list on your registry page on TheKnot.com along with all of your other registries.

Green Living   http://green-living.com
Earth-friendly and fair-trade items; they have an online registry

Greenfeet   http://www.greenfeet.com
Sustainable and eco-friendly products for the home, with an online registry

Wiliams-Sonoma   http://williams-sonoma.com
You can register for cookware that won't be harmful to you and your family (studies show some Teflon-coated pans pose a hazard). Brands to check out include Calphalon, All-Clad, and Le Creuset.

Gaiam   http://gaiam.com

Replacements, Ltd.   http://replacements.com

Organic Food Industry Information

Eat Well Guide   http://eatwellguide.org
  Resource for healthy and sustainable food

Marine Conservation Society   http://mcsuk.org

Chez Panisse   http://chezpanisse.com

Salmon Safe   http://salmonsafe.org

Organic Consumers Association   http://organicconsumers.org

Seafood Choices Alliance   http://seafoodchoices.org

EcoFish   http://www.ecofish.com

Paper Industry

Forest Stewardship Council   http://fscus.org
  Current trends and information about what is happening with
  the world's forests and the impact of paper production

Rainforest Action Network   http://ran.org
  For information about paper and sustainability

Rainforest Alliance   http://www.rainforest-alliance.org

iRethink   http://irethink.com

Funding Factory   http://fundingfactory.com

The Dogwood Alliance   http://dogwoodalliance.org

Forest Ethics   http://forestethics.org

Natural Resources Defense Council   http://nrdc.org

Paper Stationers

Joy by Mel Lim   http://joybymellim.com
  Eco-conscious paper products

Twisted Limb Paper Works   http://twistedlimbpaper.com
  Handmade 100%-recycled invitations

Baglady Designs   http://baglady-designs.com

Oblation Papers and Press   http://oblationpapers.com

Sidepony   http://sidepony.com

Printer Cartridge Recycling

We Buy Empties   http://webuyempties.com

Inkjet Cartridge   http://inkjetcartridge.com

The eCycle Group   http://ecyclegroup.com

Inkjetman   http://inkjetman.com

Ribbon

Repro Depot   http://reprodepot.com
They specialize in vintage grosgrain ribbon patterns.

Custom Paper   http://custompaper.com
A variety of ribbon, including midori, organza, dupioni.

Tourism Information

The Blue Flag Programme   http://blueflag.org
The Blue Flag is an exclusive eco-label awarded to over
3100 beaches and marinas in 36 countries across Europe,
South Africa, Morocco, New Zealand, Canada, and the
Caribbean in 2006. The Blue Flag promotes sustainable
development at beaches and marinas.

Green Globe   http://greenglobe.org
Green Globe has environmental information about international
destinations and business outlining responsible behavior across
economic, social, and environmental management. The site will
help you plan your honeymoon—the Green Globe label is used
by participating resorts, tours, and rental car companies.

Oceana   http://stopcruisepollution.com

The International Ecotourism Society
http://www.ecotourism.org

United Nations Environment Programme   http://unep.org
  Project AWARE   http://projectaware.org

Reef Relief   http://reefrelief.org

Conservation International   http://www.conservation.org

Audobon Green Leaf Eco-Rating Program
    http://www.audoboninternational.org

Transportation

Environmental car rental   http://evrental.com

Biobling   http://biobling.com
  Retrofits cars, soups them up, and makes them into biodiesel
  fuel cars (kind of like a "green" version of MTV's Pimp My Ride)

Enterprise Rent-A-Car   http://www.enterprise.com
  They rent the Toyota Prius

EVO Limo Service   http://evolimo.com
  Rent natural gas-powered limos in L.A.

Bio-Beetle   http://bio-beetle.com

Fox Rent-A-Car   http://foxrentacar.com

Travel Companies

Travelroots   http://travelroots.com
  Holidays that do good for the world

Blue Ventures   http://www.blueventures.org
  Marine Conservation Holidays

Tourism Partnership   http://tourismpartnership.org

Sustainable Travel International   http://sustainabletravel.com

Bespoke Experience   http://bespokeexperience.com

Vintage, Craft, Reusable, and Fair-Trade Items

Pixel Girlshop   http://pixelgirlshop.com
  Cute unique quirky items for favors, including notecards and
  vintage wallpaper magnets

Ex Libris Anonymous   http://bookjournals.com
  Fun, repurposed journals for useful favors

Rising Tide   http://rtfairtrade.com
  Fair-trade boutique

Taraluna Gifts   http://taraluna.com
  Fair-trade, organic gifts, and products

The Enterprising Kitchen   http://theenterprisingkitchen.org

A non-profit social service enterprise that sells handmade soaps and candles while providing workforce training to those in need

Global Crafts   http://globalcrafts.org

Handmade gifts made by craftspeople in developing countries, providing them with income-generating opportunities

A Greater Gift   http://www.agreatergift.org

Favor ideas for under $10, including a wooden box from Tibet with pretty detailing. All items are produced by local communities, and follow fair-trade practices.

EcoParti   http://ecoparti.com

Global Exchange   http://globalexchange.org

Water

BIOTA   http://biotaspringwater.com

Spring water is the world's first bottled water/beverage packaged in a Planet Friendly™ bottle.

Belu Water   http://www.belu.org

British bottled water with compostable plastic bottle made from corn; all profits go to clean-water programs.

Wedding Invitations

Invitesite   http://invitesite.com

You can customize the invitations further to make them truly one of a kind. Because you are handling the printing and the assembly, you choose the paper, and even better—these custom invitations are affordably priced.

Paporganics   http://paporganics.com

Sustainable stationery and gift wrap

Klee Paper   http://kleepaper.com

Seal-n-Send Invitations   http://www.seal-n-send.com

Sidepony   http://sidepony.com

Greg Barber Co.   http://gregbarberco.com

Eco Paper Co.   http://ecopaperco.com.au

Green Field Paper Co.   http://greenfieldpaper.com

Tree-Free Paper   http://rainforestweb.org

Wine

Amity Vineyards   http://www.amityvineyards.com

Cooper Mountain Vineyards   http://coopermountainwine.com

Frey Vineyards	http://www.freywine.com
Diamond Organics	http://diamondorganics.com
Paradigm Winery	http://www.paradigmwinery.com
Fetzer Vineyards	http://fetzer.com
The Organic Wine Company	http://theorganicwinecompany.com